THE PRESENT IN PERSPECTIVE

the
Present in

Third Edition

Perspective

A LOOK AT
THE WORLD SINCE 1945

by Hans W. Gatzke

Yale University

RAND McNALLY & COMPANY : Chicago

RAND McNALLY HISTORY SERIES

Fred Harvey Harrington, Advisory Editor

Preface

THE PURPOSE OF THIS SMALL BOOK IS TO present, in a minimum of space, the most important events that have occurred since World War II. The book is primarily written for younger readers, to whom the earlier happenings here described will seem quite remote. But even older readers may welcome this brief recapitulation, since it will help them gain a clearer perspective on current problems.

The trouble with writing "current history" is that its subject matter does not stand still. A book like this, therefore, has to be rewritten periodically. This is the third version of *The Present in Perspective*, two earlier ones having appeared in 1957 and 1961. Anyone patient enough to compare the three editions will be struck by the many important changes that have taken place in so short a time.

To present the recent past in all its complexity, events have largely been left to speak for themselves. Trends have been pointed out only where they are clearly discernible, and conclusions have been drawn only where they appear truly valid. The temptation to make predictions has been avoided. Because the book is so brief, its treatment has to be selective. Nevertheless, it is hoped that nothing vital has been overlooked or neglected.

Hans W. Gatzke

Weston, Connecticut

CONTENTS

Contents

Contents

MAPS by Vincent G. Mazzucchelli

1

FIGHTERS FOR PEACE

Dag Hammarskjold (l.), UN Secretary General, who died
in a plane crash on September 8, 1961, while
on a peace mission in the Congo. His work is being
carried on by Secretary General U Thant (r.).

UNATIONS.

THE COLD WAR

IF WE WANT TO GAIN A BETTER UNDERSTANDING of the world in which we live, we must go back at least to the end of World War II. That war has been described by some historians as the continuation or completion of the earlier great war of our century. At the end of World War I, the statesmen of Europe and the United States had met in Paris to make a peace that would prevent a repetition of the recent catastrophe. In this they had failed. Twenty years later the world became involved in a still costlier war. Given the earlier failure in 1919, one would have expected the victors in 1945 to have learned from past mistakes and to have given careful thought in advance to the kind of world they hoped to create, once the fighting was over. It is surprising, in retrospect, how little planning for peace there had been among the leaders of the Grand Alliance. These men, it seems, were too much preoccupied with winning the war to give much thought to preparations for peace. Prime Minister Winston Churchill and President Franklin D. Roosevelt had put on record some of their aims and aspirations in the Atlantic Charter in August, 1941. It was subsequently endorsed by most of the countries at war with Germany. The postwar world, the Atlantic Charter stated, was to be free from want and fear. There were to be no territorial changes against the wishes of the people concerned; each nation was to have the right to choose its own form of government; there was to be equal economic opportunity with access to essential raw materials for all nations; aggressor nations were to be disarmed; and there was to be no more use of force in the settling of international disputes.

The Atlantic Charter, however, had several shortcomings: Its tenor was idealistic and vague rather than realistic and specific; it originated early in the war, before the United States had become a belligerent, and before the shape of the postwar world could be clearly foreseen; and, most important, it was drafted without consulting the Russians, who had only recently suffered Hitler's invasion. Stalin subsequently gave qualified approval to the Atlantic Charter, but at the same time made it plain that his war aims differed considerably from the noble principles expressed therein. There were a few more top-level conferences during the war between Roosevelt and Churchill at Casablanca, Quebec, and Cairo, and between these two Western leaders and Stalin at Teheran. But these talks dealt primarily with military matters and only incidentally with long-range political issues. An exception was the meeting between Churchill and Stalin at Moscow in October, 1944. It was on this occasion that Britain recognized Russia's preeminence in Romania, Bulgaria, and Hungary, in return for comparable British control over Greece. Influence in Yugoslavia was to be divided equally between the two powers. These arrangements were not considered binding by the United States. It was not until 1945 that the problem of peace was seriously tackled. This was done at the meetings of the Big Three at Yalta and Potsdam.

THE YALTA CONFERENCE

The conference which met at the Russian resort of Yalta in the Crimea in February, 1945, is an important landmark. Its major

4

decisions concerned Germany, Poland, the Far East, and the United Nations. There had been little preliminary planning on the future of Germany. The Russians all along had insisted on a harsh settlement. The Western powers had gone along with this, and at their Quebec meeting in August, 1943, had endorsed the plan of United States Secretary of the Treasury Henry Morgenthau for the partition and de-industrialization of Germany. But since then Roosevelt and Churchill had begun to wonder if the "Morgenthau Plan" was really wise. To dismember Germany would leave a power vacuum and would greatly enhance Russia's influence in central and eastern Europe. At Yalta, therefore, the Western powers asked that final decisions on Germany's political and economic fate be postponed. Russia's demand for 10 billion dollars in reparations from Germany was referred to a Reparations Commission, which was to use Russia's figure "as a basis for discussion." Russia's request, finally, that Germany surrender to Poland the area east of the Oder and Neisse rivers was also left undecided. All that the Western Allies conceded was that Poland "must receive substantial accessions of territory in the North and West." As far as Germany was concerned, the Yalta meeting postponed rather than solved issues. The only firm agreement was on the postwar division of the country into four occupation zones (including one for France) under an Allied Control Council. The capital of Berlin, situated within the Soviet zone, was to be occupied and administered jointly; but no specific agreement was made guaranteeing Western access to the city.

Most of the time at Yalta was spent trying to establish Poland's postwar frontiers and to agree on her provisional government. The Soviet Union, for reasons of her own security, claimed a special interest in the Polish question. The fact that she was in actual possession of the country greatly strengthened her position. The problem of what territory Russia was to receive caused few difficulties. Prior to Yalta the Western leaders had already consented to the "Curzon Line" (drawn up after World War I, but subsequently ignored), and with some modifications this boundary was approved at Yalta. Russia thus received about 47 per cent of Poland's prewar territory. Her effort to compensate Poland at Germany's expense, as we have just seen, was postponed for the time being.

The real difficulty developed over the formation of Poland's future government. There were at the time two provisional governments, the Polish government-in-exile in London and the Soviet-sponsored Committee of National Liberation in Lublin. The Russians insisted that a new government be formed by enlarging the Lublin group The Western powers finally gave way on this crucial point. Their decision was made easier because the new Polish government was to hold "free and unfettered elections on the basis of universal suffrage and secret ballot." A similar promise of free elections for the other liberated peoples in central and eastern Europe was embodied in a simultaneous "Declaration on Liberated Europe." Having already resisted Soviet aims in Germany and hoping to gain Russian participation in the Pacific war and in the United Nations, the Western powers obviously shrank from making too much of an issue over a region which was so clearly within the Russian orbit.

Of all the negotiations at Yalta, those concerned with the Far East went most smoothly at the time, yet have stirred up the most criticism since. Russia's aid against Japan had been desired by the American military since shortly after Pearl Harbor and had been pledged by Stalin on several earlier occasions. But it was only at Yalta that details were worked out and that Russia was granted the concessions she expected in return for such aid. Specifically, Roosevelt agreed that the *status quo* in Outer Mongolia, already within the Russian sphere as the "Mongolian People's Republic," would be preserved; that the Kurile Islands would be transferred to the Soviet Union; and that Russian losses in the Russo-Japanese War of 1904–5 would be restored. The latter involved the return of the southern part of Sakhalin Island, the lease of the Port Arthur naval base, internationalization of the port of Dairen, and joint Russo-Chinese operation of the Chinese Eastern and South Manchurian railroads. In return, the Soviet Union promised to participate in the Pacific war and to negotiate a pact of friendship and alliance with the Chinese government of Chiang Kai-shek.

The problem closest to the heart of the American delegation at Yalta was to get British and Russian consent to final plans for a United Nations organization. The groundwork for such an organization had been laid in negotiations going back to 1941 and culminating in the Dumbarton Oaks Conference in 1944. But agreement had still to be reached on two important points: the extent of the great powers' veto in the Security Council, and the number of seats each of them was to hold in the UN Assembly. On the first of these points, the three powers had felt all along that questions involving security should be settled only by the unanimous vote of the permanent Council members, that is, the great powers. This would give each of them the power to veto any such question. The United States, in order to soften the absolute nature of such a veto, proposed that a power should not be allowed to vote in cases relating to settlements of disputes to which it might be a party. After long deliberation the British and the Russians agreed to this American modification. The issue on the second point revolved around the Soviet Union's demand that some of her constituent republics be given separate seats in the Assembly, partly to balance the membership of the British Dominions. This argument seemed plausible to Churchill, and it was agreed that at the forthcoming United Nations Conference in San Francisco the Western powers would second Russia's request for admission of the White Russian (Byelorussian) and Ukrainian republics.

These, then, were the main provisions of Yalta. They were certainly far removed from the idealistic pronouncements of the Atlantic Charter. There was some hard bargaining, but on the whole proceedings were amicable. The Yalta decisions were hailed at the time as "one of the most important steps ever taken to promote peace and happiness in the world." The success of Yalta, of course, depended on the adherence of the Soviet Union to its terms, and it was not long before they became the subject of heated controversy between East and West. But this development was not foreseen by the Western statesmen at Yalta. They and their peoples admired the Russians for their major contributions to the common war effort; and they expected the friendship born in war to facilitate the making of peace. It seemed like a good omen that America's fondest hope, the founding of a United Nations organization, was realized little more than two months after the Yalta Conference adjourned.

ORGANIZING THE UNITED NATIONS

The San Francisco Conference, which convened on April 25, 1945, was attended by delegations from fifty nations. Because of this large number of delegates, two months were needed before the Dumbarton Oaks proposals and the Yalta modifications could be made into the official United Nations Charter. In the process, many amendments were added to the original draft to give expression to the wishes of the smaller nations. But none of these affected the preponderant influence reserved for the great powers.

The Charter was signed on June 26 and went into effect on October 24, 1945. The main purposes of the United Nations, like those of the League of Nations before it, were to be the maintenance of peace and security, the development of friendly relations among nations, and the sponsorship of international cooperation in the solution of economic, social, and cultural problems. It was specifically stated, however, that the United Nations could not "intervene in matters which are essentially within the domestic jurisdiction of any state." Membership was to be open to all peace-loving states on recommendation by the Security Council and a two-thirds vote of the Assembly. During the first twenty years of the United Nations' existence more than sixty new members were admitted. The only important nonmembers at present are Switzerland, the divided states of Germany, Korea, and Vietnam, and Communist China.

The center of UN power is vested in the Security Council. Five of its eleven seats are assigned permanently to the United States, Great Britain, France, the Soviet Union, and Nationalist China. The other six members are elected, for two-year terms, by the General Assembly on recommendation of the Council. The main task of the Security Council, as the name implies, is the maintenance of peace and security. In all nonprocedural questions, unanimity of the five permanent members is required. In settling an international dispute, the Security Council can recommend a wide range of peaceful methods: mediation, arbitration, judicial settlement, and others. If its recommendations are not followed, it can suggest measures short of war, such as economic sanctions; and it may even take "such action by air, sea, or land forces as may be necessary to maintain or restore international peace." For this purpose the Charter provided for an "international police force" supplied by member nations. Such a permanent UN military force, however, has not yet been created. On the several occasions when such an army was needed—as in the Korean war, the Suez crisis, the Congo, and Cyprus—it had to be organized on a temporary basis.

The effectiveness of the Security Council, as we shall see, was increasingly hampered by disagreements between Russia and the West. Up to 1949 the Council scored a few successes in areas such as Indonesia, Israel, and Kashmir, where interests of the major powers were not in conflict. But since then the frequent use of the veto by the Soviet Union has tied the Council's hands on many crucial issues. The role thus abdicated by this basic organ has on several occasions, such as the Korean war and the Suez crisis, been assumed by the UN General Assembly. The Assembly is the most universal body of the United Nations in which all states have equal representation and equal voting power. It holds regular annual meetings, and it may be called into special session. Its decisions on important matters require a two-thirds majority; otherwise a simple majority suffices. Initially the General Assembly's functions were largely advisory, concerned with the shaping rather than the making of policy. During the Korean war, however, American initiative led to adoption of the "Uniting for Peace" resolution of November, 1950. This resolution defined the Assembly's role in times when the Security Council is deadlocked because of the veto. This attempt to strengthen the power of the United Nations has been only partly successful. In cases where the interests of the Soviet Union and the United States conflicted, as in the Hungarian revolt in 1956 and the Lebanon crisis in 1958, the UN Assembly proved little more effective than the Security Council. The Assembly's success during the Suez crisis, furthermore, was made possible only because the United States and Russia for once took a common stand on a major issue.

Still, the General Assembly has become a far more important force than the authors of the Charter had envisaged. With the expanding membership of the United Nations, the composition of the General Assembly has changed, until today the largest bloc of votes is held by the newly independent and neutralist nations of Asia and Africa. As a result, the West no longer finds it easy to command a two-thirds majority in the United Nations, and both East and West have to listen more attentively to the opinions and wishes of the nonaligned and smaller powers. Because of the needs of these powers, the emphasis of UN activity in recent years has shifted increasingly from political concerns to programs of economic and social improvement.

The purpose of the United Nations went beyond the prevention of war. To get to the roots of conflict by studying "international economic, social, cultural, educational, health, and related matters," an Economic and Social Council was set up, composed of eighteen members elected for three-year terms by the

9

General Assembly. This Council appoints its own commissions, such as the Commission on Human Rights, which in 1948 drafted the "Universal Declaration of Human Rights." The United Nations also has affiliated with it a dozen specialized agencies, such as the International Bank for Reconstruction and Development (World Bank), the International Labor Organization (inherited from the League), the World Health Organization, and the Food and Agriculture Organization. As their names indicate, most of the specialized agencies are concerned with economic matters. Beginning in 1950 the United Nations launched the very successful Expanded Program of Technical Assistance, to help economically backward countries learn new skills and make fuller use of their resources. In the cultural sphere, the United Nations Educational, Scientific, and Cultural Organization (UNESCO), with headquarters in Paris, attempts to bring about better international understanding in the arts, sciences, and education. Finally, there is the International Court of Justice at The Hague, successor to the Permanent Court of International Justice established in 1919. Its purpose is the judicial arbitration of international disputes.

The day-to-day administrative work of the United Nations is handled by its Secretariat. It is directed by a Secretary General, who is elected by the General Assembly upon the recommendation of the Security Council. The first to hold this post was Norway's foreign minister, Trygve Lie. He was succeeded in 1953 by Dag Hammarskjold of Sweden, whose wisdom, patience, and dedication in settling international disputes greatly enhanced the importance of his office. After Hammarskjold's tragic death in September, 1961, his post was assumed by U Thant of Burma, who has proved an able successor. The headquarters of the United Nations are in New York City, but occasional meetings of the General Assembly have been held in Paris.

THE POTSDAM CONFERENCE

On May 8, 1945 (V-E Day), while the San Francisco Conference was still in session, the official surrender of Germany was ratified in Berlin. The common task that had kept the Grand Alliance between East and West intact over the past years had thus been accomplished, and another top-level conference was needed to put some order into the chaos that Hitler had left behind. Already there were signs that the earlier cordiality between the Western Allies and Russia had given way to coldness and even hostility. This was chiefly due to Russia's obvious intentions of following a policy of her own in eastern Europe. Two weeks after Yalta the Soviet member of the Allied Control Council for Romania had pressured King Michael into forming a new government with strong pro-Russian leanings, a change that the United States refused to recognize. At the same time the Russians were evading the reorganization of the Lublin government in Poland and showed no signs of preparing for the free elections in that country that had been agreed on at Yalta.

The atmosphere of the Potsdam Conference in July, 1945, therefore, was quite different from that of Yalta. The fact that the first successful explosion of an atomic bomb in the proving grounds at Los Alamos, New Mexico, coincided with the beginning of the conference considerably stiffened the back of the United States delegation. With Harry S. Truman in place of Roosevelt (who had died on April 12), and Clement Attlee taking over from Churchill after the latter's defeat in Britain's parliamentary elections on July 23, Stalin remained as the only member of the original Big Three. The major agreements reached at the conference concerned the future of Germany. The Potsdam Declaration on Germany stated that the victors had no intention "to destroy or enslave the German people" but that they did intend to provide them with "the opportunity to prepare for the eventual reconstruction of their life on a democratic and peaceful basis." The aims of Allied occupation policy were specified as (1) disarmament and demilitarization; (2) denazification and the trial of war criminals; (3) democratization of Germany's political, educational, and judicial systems; (4) decentralization of her political structure and emphasis on local self-government; and (5) deindustrialization of war and heavy industries and placement of primary emphasis on agriculture and peaceful domestic industries.

Two other subjects that had already caused much trouble at Yalta continued to do so at Potsdam—Germany's eastern frontier and her payment of reparations. Without notifying her allies, Russia had already entrusted Poland with the administration of German territory east of the Oder and Neisse rivers, and had taken over the northern part of East Prussia herself. Faced with this *fait accompli*, the Western powers had no choice but to recognize "in principle . . . the ultimate transfer to the Soviet Union of the city of Königsberg and the area adjacent to it." The West insisted, however, that the final delimitation of the German-Polish frontier should wait until a definite peace settlement was reached. This did not keep Poland from expelling most of the Germans from east of the Oder-Neisse line and from claiming that the term "delimitation" merely applied to details of the frontier. Poland thus acquired almost one-fifth of Germany's pre-1938 territory. The fate of this easternmost part of Germany has remained a key issue in the cold war between East and West.

No final decision was reached at Potsdam on the total amount of German reparations, although Russia continued to insist on her lion's share of 10 billion dollars. This amount was to be collected through removal of industrial equipment from the Russian zone of occupation and from German foreign assets. In addition the Russians were to get some of the industrial equipment in the western occupation zones that was not needed for Germany's own postwar economy. The powers agreed, however, that "the amount and character of the industrial equipment unnecessary for the German peace economy and therefore available for reparations shall be made by the Control Council under policies fixed by the Allied Commission on Reparations," and that during the period of occupation Germany should be treated "as a single economic unit." Here was further cause for subsequent friction among the powers.

On other issues, the Potsdam Conference achieved very little. Russia denied Western charges that she was violating the Yalta agreements on eastern Europe and unsuccessfully tried to gain the trusteeship over one of Italy's former colonies and a voice in the control of the Turkish Straits. The only additional agreement was on the establishment of a Big Four Council of Foreign Ministers to draft the peace treaties for Germany's satellites and for Finland.

THE SURRENDER OF JAPAN

Four days after the Potsdam Conference adjourned, the United States dropped an atomic bomb on the Japanese city of Hiroshima. Two days later Soviet Russia declared war on Japan and invaded Manchuria. On August 10, 1945, after a second bomb had been dropped, Japan offered her surrender, and on August 14 (V-J Day) the war in the Far East was over. Since the United States had carried the major burden of the war against Japan, she claimed sole control over the defeated country, an arrangement that greatly facilitated the postwar administration of Japan. An Allied Council with headquarters in Tokyo, consisting of the Big Three powers and China, and a Far Eastern Commission located in Washington, composed of eleven powers primarily concerned with Far Eastern affairs, performed purely advisory functions. Supreme authority over Japanese affairs was vested in a Supreme Commander for the Allied Powers, a post held for almost six years by General Douglas MacArthur.

Since Russia had entered the war against Japan, even though only at the last moment, she was now entitled to the rights and territories she had been promised at Yalta (see p. 6). In accordance with another Yalta provision, Russia concluded a treaty of friendship and alliance with the Nationalist government of China, in which the latter agreed to the Yalta concessions as far as they affected China's interests. To complete the Far Eastern settlement, Russia and the United States jointly occupied the Korean peninsula, pending the formation of a democratic Korean government.

THE SATELLITE TREATIES

With Japan defeated, the great powers now at last could devote their full attention to the making of peace. But a successful postwar settlement required above all a certain measure of harmony among the victors, and such harmony was rapidly disappearing. It is not surprising, therefore, that the attempts of the Big Four Council of Foreign Ministers to draw up peace treaties for the European powers other than Germany and Austria soon ran into a maze of difficulties. It was not until July, 1946, that sufficient agreement had been reached on the various treaty drafts to call a meeting at Paris of the twenty-one nations that had waged war against the Axis. The Paris Conference lasted for more than two months. Like its predecessor in 1919, it was dominated entirely by the great powers; but unlike the earlier conference it gave the defeated countries an opportunity to plead their cause. Much of the time was spent in disputes between East and West, as Russia tried to impose a harsh treaty on Italy and to gain more favorable terms for those Axis satellites that were now within the Soviet sphere. By the middle of

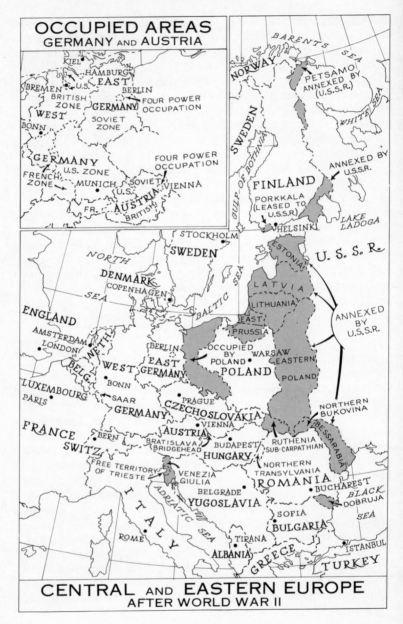

OCCUPIED AREAS
GERMANY AND AUSTRIA

CENTRAL AND EASTERN EUROPE
AFTER WORLD WAR II

December the task begun fifteen months earlier was finally completed. In view of the ever widening split between the Soviet Union
and the West, it seems surprising that any settlement was reached
at all.

The peace treaties with Italy, Romania, Hungary, Bulgaria,
and Finland were signed in the historic Clock Room of the Quai
d'Orsay on February 10, 1947. Italy, in spite of her partnership-in-
crime with Germany, got off remarkably easy, although the Italians
did not think so. She lost some territories to France, Yugoslavia,
and Greece, and her African colonies were put under the temporary
trusteeship of Great Britain, their ultimate fate to be determined
later. The port of Trieste, which Yugoslavia, with Russian backing,
was claiming for herself, was made into a free territory under the
protection of the UN Security Council. Italy's armed forces were
drastically reduced, and she agreed to pay 360 million dollars in
reparations, of which Russia was to receive 100 million. The remaining Axis satellites, as well as Finland, had to pay substantial reparations, most of which went to Russia, and also had to cut their
armed forces. With the exception of Finland these countries were
already so deeply under the influence of the Soviet Union that these
financial and military terms soon became meaningless.

Of greater interest were the territorial changes involving the
smaller powers. In the Balkans Romania lost Bessarabia (which
had been Russian from 1812 to 1918) and the northern Bucovina
(inhabited largely by Ukrainians) to the Soviet Union; but she regained northern Transylvania, which Hungary had acquired during
the war. Hungary was thus left with her 1938 frontiers, except for
a minor rectification in favor of Czechoslovakia (the Bratislava
bridgehead). Bulgaria returned her wartime gains to Yugoslavia,
but she was allowed to retain the southern Dobruja, which Romania had taken from her in 1913 and which the Axis powers had
restored to her in 1940. Another territorial change in this region,
though not part of the satellite treaties, involved the cession by
Czechoslovakia of the Ukrainian territory of Carpatho-Ruthenia to
Russia. Although most of these adjustments were based on ethnic
principles, this did not mean that the populations involved necessarily favored these changes. In the north the Russians took the
Petsamo district from Finland, thus regaining the common frontier
with Norway that had existed for centuries prior to 1918. Finland
also had to grant the Soviets a lease of the naval base at Porkkala,
which Russia relinquished again in 1956. In addition, Finland lost

15

territory along the central Russo-Finnish frontier and west of Lake Ladoga.

There were some other changes not covered by the satellite treaties that deserve mention. As far back as 1940 the Russians had incorporated the Baltic republics—Estonia, Latvia, and Lithuania—as member republics in the U.S.S.R. They were re-established as members of the Soviet Union after the Red Army reconquered the Baltic region in November, 1944, although the Western powers refused official recognition of this status. Russia's excuse was that the Baltic states had been part of the Russian Empire for two centuries before they became independent after World War I. In Europe, as in the Far East, Russia seemed bent on restoring the territorial position she had held before the advent of communism.

More important in the long run than the changes in the political map of Europe were the displacements in its human geography that took place during and directly after the war. To find anything at all comparable in Western history, we have to go back to the early Germanic migrations in the days of the late Roman Empire. Hitler had started this radical process of sorting out the ethnic confusion of eastern and central Europe by gathering the scattered German minorities of the eastern plains. By the middle of 1947, partly through Hitler's action, but mostly through expulsion after Germany's defeat, nearly ten million Germans had thus been moved or driven from regions that, in some cases, their ancestors had inhabited for centuries. In addition there were large numbers of "displaced persons" (DP's), that is, eastern Europeans who had been moved to Germany under Hitler and who now could not or would not return to their former homes. Then there were the thousands of Poles expelled from the region east of the Curzon Line and resettled in eastern Germany. And finally there were at least three hundred thousand Esths, Letts, and Lithuanians who had fled before the Red Army. The total effect of these forced population transfers, according to Arnold Toynbee, "was to cancel the ethnic effects of a thousand years of German, Polish, and Lithuanian conquest and colonization, and to restore the ethnic map to something like the *status quo ante* A.D. 1200." As the Germans were driven from cities they had founded centuries ago, these places were given Slavic names to obliterate their past. Together with the redrawing of the territorial frontiers, these population shifts have greatly simplified the ethnic picture in eastern Europe. But they have done so at a price of much human suffering and great injustice.

16

DISSENSION AMONG THE VICTORS

The signing of the satellite treaties ended, for the time being, the making of peace. Several years were to pass before similar treaties were concluded with Japan and Austria, and there has as yet been no final settlement with Germany. It is a truism that alliances go to pieces once their objectives have been achieved; and in the light of prewar differences between the Soviet Union and the West, it should have been expected that the Grand Alliance would not survive the war. Yet all the powers during the war had realized that the peaceful reorganization of the world depended on their continued collaboration. It was this belief that had led to the founding of the United Nations. Why, then, despite such awareness, did this collaboration break down?

To understand the East-West split, we must consider briefly the basically different peace aims of the two superpowers who were to play the leading roles in world affairs. American policy during the war had been to postpone major political decisions until the end of hostilities. Had some of the later issues been faced before 1943, when Russia was still on the defensive, the position of the United States in 1945 might have been stronger. The way in which most Americans, including their government, envisaged the postwar world was in prewar terms. They expected the restoration of a Europe balanced within itself, a United Nations as successor to the League of Nations, but without the latter's shortcomings, and a general adjustment among the victors, insuring to each equitable spheres of political and economic influence in which the enlightened principles of the Atlantic Charter and the United Nations would gradually be realized.

But the total defeat of the Axis made a return to the past quite impossible. The collapse of Germany and Japan left a power vacuum in Europe and the Far East that had to be filled. America's role in the Far Eastern war predestined her for a leading position in that part of the world, and the United States never hesitated to assume this responsibility. In Europe, on the other hand, the situation was different. America's traditional aversion to involvement in the affairs of the old continent was still a strong factor in her immediate postwar policy. This attitude was shown in the popular clamor for "getting the boys home" as soon as the fighting was over; and it was reflected in such governmental measures as the abrupt ending of Lend-Lease operations in the summer of 1945.

17

There was to be American participation, of course, in the occupation of Germany and Austria, and America's role in the United Nations certainly was a radical departure from her isolationist retreat after World War I. But there was still no clear understanding of the deep effect which the collapse of Germany and the emergence of Russia had upon the European balance of power. The fact that Britain and France, while still "great powers" by courtesy, were no match for the Soviet Union and needed the active support of the United States to maintain that balance, was only realized gradually, as the divergence of aims between Russia and the West became ever more obvious.

While America's immediate policy in Europe was one of partial withdrawal, the policy of the Soviet Union was the direct opposite. Russia's professed aims were economic reconstruction with the aid of large-scale reparations, and the creation of a security sphere in eastern Europe that would prevent the recurrence of an invasion from the west. These aims, the Russians felt, had been recognized at Yalta and Potsdam. There was an additional requirement for Russian security, however, never clearly stated, and that was the establishment of governments friendly to the Soviet Union along her western frontier. This was the real source of much of the subsequent friction, because in Russian eyes a government to be friendly had to be pro-Communist. In retrospect, of course, this all seems quite obvious. But it did not appear so at the end of the war. It took the object lesson of Poland to drive home to the West the fundamental differences between its own and Russia's concept of what constituted a "democratic" government. And it soon became clear that the West was unwilling to recognize Russian predominance in eastern Europe if this was synonymous with the spread of communism in that area.

Here, then, was the basic issue: What the West looked upon as Communist expansion, Russia defended on grounds of national security. There is some doubt whether Stalin himself foresaw the extent to which the nations of eastern Europe ultimately became communized. Certain is that Stalin felt a clear delimitation of spheres of influence had been arrived at between the East and West. He thus abstained from interfering with England's efforts to deal with the threat of communism in Greece (see p. 23); yet at the same time he refused to tolerate interference with Russia's efforts to insure the victory of communism in Poland. Russia's desire for security, however, was not satisfied with the domination of eastern Europe. Since Russia was most deeply concerned over the resurgence of a powerful Germany, the establishment of a friendly, that is, a Communist, regime in that country came to be the Soviet Union's foremost aim. It was largely over the German issue that the dissension among the victors developed into a cold war of ever widening dimensions.

THE EAST-WEST SPLIT OVER GERMANY

The German Reich had been divided into four occupation zones, with an Allied Control Council in Berlin to insure a uniform policy. But when the powers tried to cope with Germany's economic and political problems, they soon discovered a considerable divergence of aims. The Russians, having suffered most heavily, immediately began collecting large reparations in kind from their zone. They also insisted on an additional share of reparations from the rest of Germany. The Soviet zone was closed against inspection by the Western powers, and its economy was gradually nationalized. Politically, the Soviet zone was the first to see the revival of a German party system. To make sure of a favorable majority, the Russians forced the large Socialist Party to merge with the less numerous Communists into the "Socialist Unity Party" (SED). For the future the Soviet Union favored a centralized German state, to facilitate its eventual communization.

The French, like the Russians, were determined to make the Germans pay for the war and to prevent Germany from ever again disturbing the peace. But, unlike the Soviets, France saw the best guarantee for future security in a loose federal union rather than in a centralized state. Any early efforts of the Allied Control Council to treat the country as an economic or political entity were therefore vetoed by the Council's French representative. Only after the East-West split over Germany had become irreparable did the French gradually join the Anglo-American side.

Britain and the United States, while differing on some details, agreed on their basic principles in dealing with Germany. Since their zones were more heavily populated, they not only had to support their own occupation forces (while the French and Russians lived off the country) but also had to import large quantities of food to keep the Germans alive. Both England and America initially favored the dismantling of German factories and the

19

breaking-up (decartelization) of large enterprises such as the Krupp armament works and the I. G. Farben chemical combine. But in time both powers realized that the only way in which West Germany's large population could help support itself was by increasing, rather than decreasing, her industrial production and by treating Germany as the "single economic unit" that had been agreed on at Potsdam. The main exponent of this revised Western attitude toward Germany was General Lucius Clay, commander of the American zone during the most crucial postwar years until 1949. In the political sphere, the Western powers favored a federated, rather than a centralized, German state.

As this brief summary shows, there was considerable disagreement among the British and Americans on the one hand and the French as well as the Russians over the policies they advocated for Germany. Further disagreement arose over denazification. Each power soon began accusing the others of not doing enough to eliminate former Nazis from positions of influence. Considering the large number of persons who had been involved in the activities of the Nazi Party, complete denazification was a stupendous task. The United States made the most thorough attempt, but finally had to turn the job over to the Germans themselves, with not very satisfactory results. In all four zones Nazis who were not convicted of actual crimes gradually began to reassert themselves.

The first major showdown between the East and West came over German reparations. When the Russians refused to abide by the Potsdam terms governing the removal of industrial equipment, the British and Americans in May, 1946, stopped the delivery of reparations from their zones. At the same time Anglo-American leaders demanded that Germany be treated as an economic unit and that some general plan be devised for her economic future. When both the French and the Russians objected, Britain and the United States in December, 1946, joined their zones into an economic "Bizonia." By early 1947 the four-power administration of Germany had come to a virtual standstill. In an effort to break this deadlock, the Big Four Council of Foreign Ministers met in Moscow in March, 1947. Just about this time American foreign policy, under the direction of Secretary of State George C. Marshall, began taking a noticeably firmer line, expressed in the so-called Truman Doctrine (see p. 23). The effect of its proclamation upon the Moscow meeting was to make an already strained atmosphere still more tense. American and British efforts to reach agreement on German economic unity again ran into Russian and French opposition, and after six weeks of futile wrangling the conference adjourned.

The failure of the Moscow Conference and the proclamation of the Truman Doctrine are usually considered to have marked the beginning of the cold war. From now on actions and counteractions, not only in Germany but elsewhere, followed one another in rapid succession. And each such action further intensified the climate of mutual distrust between East and West. As far as Germany was concerned, the months following the Moscow meeting saw the Russian and Western zones drifting further and further apart. In June, 1947, Secretary Marshall announced his plan for the economic rehabilitation of Europe (see p. 23). To improve the economic situation of West Germany as part of western European recovery, the Anglo-American commanders raised the industrial level of Bizonia, especially the output of steel. This action brought forth a tirade of abuse from the East against the "imperialist" policy of the West. In October, 1947, the Russians founded the "Cominform" as a central organization of international communism, with a pronounced anti-Western platform. Three weeks later General Clay lifted the ban against attacks on communism in the West German press. When the Council of Foreign Ministers met again in London in December, 1947, the atmosphere was one of open hostility. The meeting broke up after three weeks of fruitless argument.

In the meantime, events in East and West Germany continued to move along their separate ways. In an effort to halt the creation of a West German state, the Soviet authorities in June, 1948, imposed a tight blockade on the western sectors of the city of Berlin, claiming that with the end of the four-power government there was no further need for the Western powers to remain in the former German capital. The Americans replied with an unprecedented airlift and by imposing a counterblockade on East Germany. The duel over Berlin ended in the spring of 1949, when the Russians, realizing the impossibility of ousting the Western powers, lifted the blockade.

The division of Germany, meanwhile, had progressed further. A West German Parliamentary Council on May 8, 1949, adopted the Basic Law of the future "Federal Republic of Germany." Simultaneously the East German People's Congress completed a constitution for the "German Democratic Republic." In mid-August, 1949, the first general elections were held in West Germany, and within a month the Federal Republic had been launched. In October, 1949, the Democratic Republic was established in the East, without the benefit of popular elections. In November the newly named "high commissioners" of the three Western powers, and the chancellor of West Germany, Konrad Adenauer, signed the Petersberg agreement, which defined the rights of the occupying powers. The struggle between East and West over Germany had reached a stalemate—Germany was split in two.

THE COLD WAR IN EUROPE

Germany was not the only scene of East-West conflict. It was the creeping expansion of communism in eastern and southeastern Europe that caused the United States to take the lead in drawing together the nations of the West, first economically and later militarily. The communization of eastern Europe was a gradual process. Using her occupation forces to discourage opposition, the Soviet Union in the course of three years was able to weld the nations within her orbit into a solidly Communist bloc. By early 1947 this development was causing the deepest alarm in the West. Romania, Poland, Yugoslavia, Albania, and Bulgaria all had either Communist or pro-Communist regimes; Czechoslovakia had a coalition government headed by a Communist; and in Hungary a purge against anti-Communists within the coalition government was under way. In addition, the Communists had emerged as the strongest party in the French National Assembly and the third strongest party in the Italian Constituent Assembly. What could the Western powers do to stem this rising Communist tide, without starting a third world war?

A partial answer to this question had already been given in an address by Winston Churchill at Fulton, Missouri, in March, 1946. "From Stettin in the Baltic to Trieste in the Adriatic," its most memorable passage ran, "an iron curtain has descended across the continent." The former British prime minister strongly condemned "the police governments" of eastern Europe and recommended a policy of strength as the only attitude the Russians respected. Churchill's call for resistance to Russia was echoed in the American State Department. George F. Kennan, head of the department's policy-planning staff, declared that "the main element of any

United States policy toward the Soviet Union must be that of a long-term, patient but firm and vigilant application of counter-force at a series of constantly shifting geographical and political points." The occasion for publicly proclaiming the "containment" policy as the basis of American action came in the spring of 1947, when Russian influence threatened to reach toward the Mediterranean by way of Greece and Turkey.

Greece, since the end of World War II, had been sharply divided between a militant left and a royalist right. Britain, concerned over her interests in the eastern Mediterranean, had tried to stabilize the situation by backing the rightists, who won the first postwar elections in March, 1946. But the return of the monarchy did not end Greek unrest. The Communist contingent, supported by Greece's neighbors, started extensive guerilla activities, which soon developed into a civil war. The only way for the government to hold its own was through continued British aid. But Britain was having her own economic difficulties at home. In addition, she had also been supporting Turkey's efforts to resist Soviet demands for territorial concessions in the Caucasus and control of the Turkish Straits. In the spring of 1947, therefore, Britain felt she could no longer afford aid to Greece and Turkey and announced its termination. At this point the United States stepped into the breach.

On March 12, 1947, President Truman, in a speech to Congress, declared that it should be the policy of the United States "to support free peoples who are resisting attempted subjugation by armed minorities or by outside pressures." He asked for the appropriation of 400 million dollars in economic and military aid to Greece and Turkey and for authorization to send American military and civilian personnel to those countries. Here was a wholly new concept in American foreign policy, soon to be known as the "Truman Doctrine." American help, President Truman said, was to be "primarily through economic and financial aid." This idea was elaborated upon in an address by Secretary of State Marshall, on June 5, 1947, at Harvard University. The "Marshall Plan," which was thus inaugurated, called for far-reaching economic assistance to European nations. It was motivated both by humanitarianism and by national self-interest. By helping Europe to help itself, America hoped to bring about a general recovery that would banish the threat of communism.

The reaction of Europe to this imaginative American proposal showed how far the continent had already become divided along ideological lines. The nations of western Europe responded with enthusiasm. A central agency, the Organization for European Economic Cooperation (OEEC), was formed in the spring of 1948 to supervise what was called the European Recovery Program (ERP). Within the four years of ERP operation, thanks to Europe's energy and 13 billion American dollars, the Marshall Plan not only prevented the economic collapse of western Europe but raised production and living standards in many countries above prewar levels. As far as Russia was concerned, the plan was branded as another step in America's policy of establishing an anti-Communist, capitalist alliance. There was nothing in Secretary Marshall's proposal to exclude the nations of eastern Europe from participation. But Russian pressure soon forced any satellite that was attracted to America's generous offer back into line. In January, 1949, a Council for Mutual Economic Assistance ("Molotov Plan") was formed in Moscow, as an Eastern counterpart to ERP.

By this time, however, Russia had taken other steps to tighten her hold over eastern Europe. Before the end of the war she had already concluded mutual assistance pacts with Yugoslavia, Poland, and Czechoslovakia. Since then the Soviets had signed similar treaties with Hungary, Romania, Bulgaria, and Finland. In September, 1947, at a conference in Warsaw, the Communist parties of eastern Europe, together with those of France and Italy, founded the Communist Information Bureau (Cominform). Its purpose (as was that of its predecessor, the Comintern, which had been dissolved in 1943) was to coordinate the activities of European communism and to combat "Anglo-American imperialism."

The most serious blow to the cause of freedom, however, was struck in February, 1948, when the Communists in a *coup d'état* seized the government of Czechoslovakia. That small republic had tried to steer a middle course between the East and West. In their foreign policy the Czechs had followed the lead of the Soviet Union, whose fear of Germany they shared. But in her domestic affairs Czechoslovakia had tried to maintain some of the freedoms that had made her an outpost of Western democracy in the interwar period. In the elections of May, 1946, however, the Communists had polled 38 per cent of the vote, and Communist Klement Gottwald had become head of a coalition government. By the spring of 1948 the Communists, with Soviet support, had so strengthened their position that they could force President Beneš

24

to agree to a predominantly Communist regime. In March, 1948, Foreign Minister Jan Masaryk, known for his Western leanings, committed suicide. In June President Beneš resigned and was succeeded by Gottwald. Except for Finland, all of eastern Europe was now in Communist hands.

The Communist seizure of Czechoslovakia was only the latest example of postwar Soviet expansionism, and there were signs that it might not be the last. The Western powers, therefore, decided that more drastic measures were needed to contain the Russians. In March, 1947, France and Great Britain had concluded a military alliance, the Treaty of Dunkirk. To widen its scope and effectiveness, these two powers, together with the Benelux countries— Belgium, the Netherlands, and Luxembourg—in March, 1948, signed the Treaty of Brussels. It called for a fifty-year alliance against armed attack in Europe and established a Western Union for mutual cooperation in economic and military matters. Western Europe, without American assistance, however, was no match for the military might of the Red Army. The United States was aware of this and in 1948 began discussions for a wider alliance. The North Atlantic Treaty was signed in Washington on April 4, 1949, by the members of the Brussels pact plus Italy, Portugal, Denmark, Iceland, Norway, Canada, and the United States. These twelve powers were joined later by Greece and Turkey (1951) and by West Germany (1955). The gist of the treaty was contained in Article 5, which stated that "an armed attack against one or more" of its members, in Europe, North Africa, or North America, "shall be considered an attack against them all." A North Atlantic Council was set up to direct the formation of the North Atlantic Treaty Organization (NATO). General Dwight D. Eisenhower was appointed as NATO Supreme Commander in December, 1950, and established his headquarters at Rocquencourt, France, the following April. To provide the necessary financial aid, the American Congress approved a Mutual Defense Assistance Program which by 1959 had appropriated more than 10 billion dollars.

Nato . France, G.B. Bel, Neth, Lunem, Italy, Portug, Denm. Iceland, Nor. Can. U.S.

THE UNITED NATIONS IN THE COLD WAR

In the course of two years, from 1947 to 1949, America's foreign policy had thus undergone a major reorientation. Up to 1947 the United States had hoped that the system of collective security embodied in the United Nations would suffice to cope with international crises. Experience soon taught otherwise. Collective security was not very effective as long as one power, through use of the veto, could prevent the others from taking the necessary measures. This regrettable situation did not mean that the West abandoned or ignored the United Nations. On the contrary, special care was taken that the regional pacts concluded among the Western powers did not conflict with but rather supplemented the UN Charter.

The United Nations had no sooner started its first session in January, 1946, than it received a complaint from Iran against the Soviet Union. To counteract German influence, British and Russian forces had occupied that oil-rich Middle Eastern country in 1941. Both powers had promised to withdraw their forces at the end of the war. When the time came, the Russians refused to leave. At this point the Security Council was asked to intervene. By putting pressure on the Soviet Union, the Council finally got Russia to withdraw. This was the first modest achievement of the United Nations in settling an international issue.

There were other disputes that came before the United Nations during its early years. As long as such disputes did not involve the major powers, the United Nations, like the League of Nations before it, was quite effective. In 1947 the Security Council called for a cease-fire between Dutch and native forces in Indonesia and initiated negotiations that led to the independence of the Republic of Indonesia. In 1948 the Security Council helped stop the fighting between India and Pakistan over Kashmir. But when it came to settling conflicts between small powers that were backed by Russia or the United States, the United Nations found its work much more difficult.

This was shown in the case of Greece. That unhappy country, as we have seen, was plagued by civil war. In December, 1946, Greece complained to the United Nations that Yugoslavia, Bulgaria, and Albania were aiding the Greek Communists. A commission appointed by the Security Council found the Greek charges to be correct. But Russia used her veto to prevent the Council from taking further action. To break the deadlock, the Greek question, in October, 1947, was referred to the General Assembly. But it was chiefly due to American aid and the defection of Yugoslavia from the Communist camp in early 1948 (see p. 116) that the Greek government finally gained the upper hand in its fight against communism.

In the Greek crisis the role of the United Nations had been greatly overshadowed by the actions of the major powers. In the solution of the Palestine problem, where Russia and the United States saw eye to eye, the United Nations played a more decisive part. The idea of making Palestine a Jewish state originated with the Zionist movement at the end of the nineteenth century. During World War I Great Britain, in the "Balfour Declaration," had favored Zionist aspirations, as long as they did not "prejudice the civil and religious rights of existing non-Jewish communities in Palestine." After World War I Palestine became the mandate of Great Britain under the League of Nations. Encouraged by the Balfour Declaration, large numbers of Jews migrated to the Holy Land, especially after the advent of Hitler in 1933. This influx alarmed the Arabs, who had inhabited the region for centuries. To prevent losing Arab support in the vital Middle East, Britain in 1939 imposed restrictions on Jewish migration to Palestine and in 1945 prohibited immigration altogether. But large-scale illegal immigration continued, and the British found it increasingly difficult to keep order between Jews and Arabs. Various proposals for a compromise satisfied neither side. In April, 1947, Britain referred the matter to the United Nations and announced her intention to withdraw from Palestine in May, 1948.

The United Nations decided that the most feasible solution would be the partition of Palestine. But while this was acceptable to the Jews, it did not satisfy the Arabs. When the British withdrew, a Jewish provisional government under David Ben-Gurion proclaimed the independent state of Israel. Both the United States and Russia immediately recognized the new regime. But soon the sporadic fighting between Jews and Arabs developed into a full-scale war. The Israeli forces gained the upper hand and cleared their new country of Arab armies. United Nations efforts to secure an armistice did not succeed until July, 1949. Even then the armistice remained an uneasy one, with constant border clashes threatening to flare up into a new war. The Arab countries refused to recognize Israel, and more than eight hundred thousand Arab refugees, made homeless by the Arab-Israeli war, helped keep the Palestine issue alive (see p. 163).

Among other major problems facing the United Nations from the beginning was disarmament. A Commission for Conventional Armaments was formed to discuss this question. But it soon decided that the international situation, for the time being at least, made any control of traditional weapons impossible. The chief con-

27

cern, however, was over the atomic bomb. To discover ways and means of controlling atomic energy and restricting atomic weapons, an Atomic Energy Commission was created in January, 1946. At its first session the United States representative on the Commission, Bernard M. Baruch, presented his country's plan for atomic control. It called for the establishment of an International Atomic Development Authority with a monopoly over all raw materials and processes concerned with atomic energy. The plan provided the Authority with the right of inspection, in order to insure the use of atomic energy for peaceful purposes only. The United States promised to hand over to the Authority its atomic knowledge and facilities and to destroy its supply of atomic weapons once the system of control and inspection had become effective. Since America still held a monopoly in the atomic field, this was a generous offer. But the Soviet Union opposed any inspection by the proposed Authority and suggested instead inspection by the Security Council, whose actions were subject to the veto. The Russians also demanded that the United States destroy its stockpile of atomic bombs before any control system went into effect. Despite the subsequent indorsement of the "Baruch Plan" by an overwhelming majority of the General Assembly, the Soviet veto in the Security Council prevented its adoption. In July, 1949, the Atomic Energy Commission voted to end its deliberations until a basis for agreement among the major powers could be found. Two months later the world was startled by reports of an atomic explosion inside the Soviet Union. With both sides now in possession of this terrible weapon, agreement on atomic control had become more imperative but also more difficult.

Taken as a whole, the efforts of the United Nations during its early years to maintain peace and security were not very successful. The main achievements of the United Nations were in the less spectacular social and economic fields. These absorbed the main energy of its more than three thousand staff members and its many special agencies. In December, 1948, the General Assembly initiated a long-range program of technical assistance to the world's underdeveloped areas. Such a plan, to be effective, needed the help of the richest and technically most advanced nation, the United States. In his inaugural address in January, 1949, President Truman rose to the occasion. He outlined four points of future policy, the last of which called for "a bold new program for making the benefits of our scientific advances and industrial progress available for the improvement and growth of underdeveloped areas." This was the beginning of the Point Four Program. It was aided by American money and personnel. The U.S.S.R. and her satellites refused to participate in Point Four, but in time started their own program of aid to underdeveloped countries.

Despite these positive achievements, it was by no means certain that the United Nations would be able to perform its primary function: the prevention of war and the punishment of aggressor nations. To test the effectiveness of the world organization, a major international incident was needed. Such an incident arose in the summer of 1950 with the sudden invasion of South Korea by North Korean forces.

THE COLD WAR IN THE FAR EAST

In dealing with the cold war in the Far East, we must keep in mind the radical changes taking place in Asia since World War II: the emergence of most of Asia's former colonial peoples into political independence (see Chapter 5). The international effects of this transformation were not really felt until the cold war was well under way. When these effects did appear, it soon become clear that most of the new nations of Asia were unwilling to be drawn into the East-West conflict. They preferred instead to remain neutral.

The first problem facing the victors in the Far East concerned the future of Japan. As we have seen, the United States claimed a dominant voice in the future of that country. For this reason the tensions that arose in Europe over the joint occupation of Germany were avoided in the Far East. The occupation of Japan was directed by General Douglas MacArthur. He approached his task with firmness and tact and achieved a remarkable success in a short time. The directive given him called for complete disarmament and demilitarization, the development of democratic institutions, and the creation of a viable economy. In pursuing these objectives, MacArthur was to work through the emperor and his government rather than through a hierarchy of military government, as was done in Germany. This arrangement, too, facilitated matters.

As a result of the war, Japan was reduced from an empire of 3 million square miles and 500 million people to the 142,000 square miles she had ruled a century ago, when Japan was first brought into contact with the outside world. But while at that time there were only about 28 million Japanese, today there are close to 100 million. To support this large population in an area about the size of California is Japan's major problem. In the early days of occupation, attempts were made to break up the large family combinations of industrial and financial power (*zaibatsu*) and to divide the large landholdings of absentee landlords. The right of collective bargaining was recognized, and labor unions were organized. But the breaking up of large corporations was slowed down as detrimental to Japan's recovery, and for the same reason the right to strike was curbed. The redistribution of land, on the other hand, proceeded, and by 1952, 90 per cent of the arable acreage was owned by former tenants. Despite these reforms, however, Japan required close to 2 billion dollars of American aid in the first six years after the war. It was only with the demand for strategic goods during the Korean war that Japan's economy began to show any marked improvement.

The problems of demilitarization and democratization proved much simpler. The Japanese imperial army and navy were dissolved, patriotic organizations were banned, and education was purged of its militaristic elements. Emperor Hirohito disclaimed the divinity attributed to him by his people and denied the idea of Japanese racial superiority. To aid the democratization of Japan, a new constitution was proclaimed in 1947. It was closely modeled on the democratic institutions of Great Britain. Sovereignty was transferred from the emperor to the people, individual rights were safeguarded, and women were given equal status with men. Early postwar elections brought large Socialist returns, but by 1948 a swing to the right set in, paralleling a similar trend in economic affairs.

By 1950 the occupation had accomplished most of its aims, and the time had come to conclude a peace treaty. The rift between the United States and Russia, however, made a peace conference impracticable. Instead, the United States took matters into its own hands, preparing a peace treaty which was signed on September 8, 1951. The treaty restored Japanese sovereignty, but only over the four main islands. There were no military or economic restrictions, except that the United States was permitted to maintain military bases in Japan. America also gained trusteeship over the Ryukyu and Bonin islands and over Japan's former Pacific mandates. Japan relinquished the Kurile Islands and southern Sakhalin (all of them already occupied by Russia) as well as Formosa; but their future disposition was left open. It was a purposely generous treaty, which recognized the value of Japan as an ally against communism. For this reason the Soviet Union refused to sign it. Some of Japan's neighbors, especially the Philippines, Australia, and New Zealand, also felt apprehensive about a possible military revival of Japan. To allay their fears, the United States signed a mutual security treaty with the Philippines and a similar pact with Australia and New Zealand (ANZUS Treaty). In addition, the United States and Japan signed a bilateral defense agreement which in 1952 was broadened into a mutual security pact. Japan thus became America's main bastion in the struggle with Russia for influence in the Far East.

If in Japan matters went largely according to American wishes, in China developments were much less favorable. The end of the war found China still divided between the Nationalist forces of Chiang Kai-shek and the Communist forces of Mao Tse-tung. Chiang had the support of powerful Chinese business and banking circles. Mao Tse-tung's program of land reform gave him the backing of China's landless millions. Both groups embarked on a campaign for the regions liberated from the Japanese. In this contest the Communists were the more successful. Various attempts to end the Chinese civil war by mediation proved fruitless. In the course of 1948 the decline of Chiang Kai-shek's forces, already evident in 1947, proceeded rapidly, and by the end of the year most of northern China was in Communist hands. The Nationalists by now had lost most of their best troops. Corruption among their provincial leaders had led to surrender or sale to the Communists of vast amounts of equipment that had been supplied by the United States. The Nationalist economy, badly in need of reform, had long depended on American aid, which since V-J Day had exceeded 2 billion dollars. But as time went on and the Nationalist government failed to reform itself, American aid was drastically curtailed and finally, in August, 1949, completely cut off. A few months earlier Chiang Kai-shek had begun the withdrawal of his forces to the island of Formosa. The Nationalist capital, Nanking, fell in April, 1949, Shanghai in May, and Canton in October. By early 1950 the whole mainland of China was in Communist hands. On October 1, 1949, the People's Republic of China was proclaimed at Peiping. The new regime was immedi-

31

ately recognized by the Soviet Union, but not by the United States. To the latter, the victory of communism in China was a major setback. Its importance was brought home almost immediately as developments in Korea transformed the hitherto cold war in that country into an armed conflict, involving not only the United States, but ultimately Communist China as well.

THE KOREAN WAR

The great powers had agreed that Korea, originally part of China, but in Japanese hands since 1910, should be given her independence after the war. At Yalta and Potsdam it was decided to divide the Korean peninsula, for purposes of temporary occupation, along the thirty-eighth parallel, with the United States assuming responsibility for the southern half, and the U.S.S.R. for the northern half. The result of this partition for Korea, as for Germany, was the creation of two widely different native regimes. The Russians set up a Communist-dominated Provisional People's Committee, which catered to the poor peasants. The Americans in their zone favored the propertied, conservative elements. American efforts to bring about a merger of the two zones on the basis of free elections were countered by Russian proposals for the withdrawal of all occupation forces. When no agreement was reached, the matter was referred to the United Nations in early 1948, where the American proposal for elections was adopted. Since the Russians refused to let their zone participate, the elections were limited to the south, where they resulted in a conservative, rightist victory. After continued refusal by North Korea to join the National Assembly in the south, a Republic of Korea was proclaimed in August, 1948, with Dr. Syngman Rhee as president. A month later the North Koreans formed their own People's Democratic Republic. In December, 1948, the Soviet Union announced the withdrawal of its forces from North Korea. Six months later America followed suit in the south. A UN commission continued its efforts to mediate between the two regions, but with negative results. In September, 1949, the commission warned of a possible civil war in Korea.

On June 24, 1950, North Korean troops, spearheaded by Russian-built tanks, crossed the thirty-eighth parallel in order to "liberate" South Korea. The UN Security Council immediately called upon North Korea to cease hostilities and withdraw. When the North Koreans refused to comply, the Council asked members of the United Nations to give assistance to the Republic of Korea. The United States had already decided to intervene, and was subsequently joined by token forces from other UN members. General MacArthur was placed in command of the operation. The United Nations had passed a major landmark. For the first time in its brief history, it had decided to use force. This move was made possible only because of Russia's temporary boycott of the Security Council, due to the United Nations' refusal to admit Communist China in place of Nationalist China. The Soviet Union consequently called the UN action illegal, and together with Communist China accused the United States of aggression against North Korea.

The war in Korea started off badly for the forces of the United Nations. Heavily outnumbered and inadequately equipped, the UN army had to beat a hasty retreat, and by early August, 1950, was confined to a small defensive perimeter around the port of Pusan in the southeastern corner of Korea. From there, beginning in September, General MacArthur in a brilliant counteroffensive cleared South Korea and drove the invaders across the thirty-eighth parallel toward the Yalu River, the border between North Korea and Communist China. At this point the war entered its crucial phase. Warnings from Red China and the presence of Chinese "volunteers" among North Korean forces had for some time raised the possibility of Chinese intervention. General MacArthur apparently did not believe that the Chinese would enter the war, or he was convinced that if they did, they could be beaten. In November, therefore, he launched a major drive toward the Yalu River, with the intention of ending the Korean war. Two days later massive Chinese forces intervened and within the next few weeks drove the UN armies back across the thirty-eighth parallel, inflicting terrible losses. By the spring of 1951 the UN forces had slugged their way back to the thirty-eighth parallel, and there they remained, locked in a seemingly hopeless stalemate with their far more numerous Korean and Chinese adversaries.

The controversy over how to break this deadlock threw the United States into a violent domestic crisis, culminating in the dismissal of General MacArthur by President Truman in April, 1951 (see p. 78). MacArthur was succeeded by General Matthew Ridgway. In the summer of 1951 negotiations between United

Nations and Chinese representatives for a cease-fire were begun at Panmunjom. Yet it took two more years of fighting and negotiating, with interminable haggling over the exchange of prisoners, before an agreement was finally signed on July 27, 1953. After thirty-seven months of fighting, costing more than 54,000 American lives and 22 billion dollars, the Korean war ended where it had begun, at the thirty-eighth parallel; and it ended not in victory, but in a mere truce.

THE CLIMAX OF THE COLD WAR

Korea was not the only theater of conflict between the free and Communist worlds in the Far East. After the Korean war bogged down into a stalemate, Communist pressure shifted to Indochina (see p. 156). There were other scenes of more "peaceful" Communist expansion. In 1951 Tibet was subjected to the domination of Communist China; Southeast Asia experienced a continuous series of Communist disturbances; and elsewhere in the world any former colonial people rebelling against the West could count on Communist support. Russia's relations with Communist China continued to be close, the two having signed a thirty-year pact of friendship and mutual assistance in 1950; and the Soviet hold over the satellite countries of eastern Europe appeared unshakable.

The West, meanwhile, was busy stepping up its defenses. Armed forces everywhere were increased until the gross imbalance between East and West was substantially reduced. America's military budget was increased from an average of 14 billion dollars per year before 1950 to 21 billion dollars in 1951. American foreign aid was increasingly directed into military channels. NATO was perfected into a closely coordinated defense mechanism. Regional alliances were extended to other parts of the world with the Tripartite Security Treaty (ANZUS Treaty) of 1951, the Southeast Asia Treaty of 1954, and the Middle East Treaty of 1955. The latter two treaties, although signed during the period of coexistence after 1953, nevertheless were repercussions from the shock caused by the invasion of South Korea in 1950. Not only did the West consolidate its existing forces, it also cast about for new allies. With the conclusion of the Japanese Peace Treaty in 1951 and the subsequent United States–Japanese defense agreement, an American foothold was gained in the Far East. In Europe the inte-

ALLIANCES OF THE UNITED STATES

Regional Treaties

Organization of American States (OAS)—1947

Argentina	Dominican Republic	Nicaragua
Bolivia	Ecuador	Panama
Brazil	El Salvador	Paraguay
Chile	Guatemala	Peru
Colombia	Haiti	United States
Costa Rica	Honduras	Uruguay
Cuba (excluded in 1962)	Mexico	Venezuela

North Atlantic Treaty Organization (NATO)—1949

Belgium	Greece (1951)	Portugal
Canada	Iceland	Turkey (1951)
Denmark	Italy	United Kingdom
France	Luxembourg	United States
German Federal	Netherlands	
Republic (1955)	Norway	

Tripartite Security Treaty (ANZUS)—1951

Australia	New Zealand	United States

Southeast Asia Treaty Organization (SEATO)—1954

Australia	Pakistan	United Kingdom
France	Philippines	United States
New Zealand	Thailand	

**Central Treaty Organization (CENTO),
formerly Middle East Treaty Organization (METO)—1955**

Iran	Pakistan	United Kingdom
Iraq (until 1959)	Turkey	United States (1959)

Bilateral Treaties

United States—Philippines   1951
United States—Japan   1951, 1960
United States—Republic of Korea   1953
United States—Republic of China   1954

gration of West Germany into NATO (1955) similarly strengthened the Western position. Further Western gains were derived from the rapprochement between Yugoslavia and the West after 1950, and from the treaty between the United States and Spain in 1953.

While both East and West were thus avidly working for a military balance of power, developments in the atomic field gave new urgency to what otherwise would have been merely a traditional race for armaments and alliances. With the explosion of an atomic bomb in the Soviet Union in September, 1949, the atomic race was on. In 1952 America tipped the balance by testing the first hydrogen weapon; but the next year the Soviet Union again caught up with the United States by producing its own H-bomb. The cold war was clearly headed for a climax. If a major show-down involving the atomic strength of Russia and the United States was avoided at that critical time, the reason was that the suicidal folly of a nuclear war had already become all too obvious. It was the realization that war as a means of settling international disputes was ruled out which made leaders on both sides explore the possibility of finding a modus vivendi. The atomic stalemate and the death of Stalin in May, 1953, ushered in a new phase in the cold war. Before we discuss these years of "competitive coex-istence," we must take a look at the internal developments in the world's major areas.

2

YOUTH FOR EUROPEAN UNITY

A group of young Germans protesting General de Gaulle's
veto of Great Britain's admission to the
Common Market. The signs read: "We want unity,
not grandeur!" and "Europe doesn't want a Führer!"

WIDE WORLD PHOTOS.

THE REASSERTION
OF WESTERN
EUROPE

ONE OF THE MOST SIGNIFICANT RESULTS OF
World War II has been the decline of Europe's pre-eminence in
world affairs. The fate of the old continent in our day has come
to be determined more and more by two superpowers, originally
descendent, but by now quite independent, from Europe. Europe's
decline had already been evident in World War I, which would
have ended quite differently had it not been for the intervention
of the United States. But when, after 1919, America returned to
her traditional policy of isolation, a semblance of the old European
system of great powers was resurrected and survived for a brief
spell between the wars. It was during this period that the second
of the superpowers, the Soviet Union, began to show some of the
great potentialities which have been fulfilled in our time, and
began to secede from the traditional Europe of which Russia had
once been a part. As a result of Communist expansion since World

39

War II, the political and cultural sphere of Europe today no longer corresponds to its geographic boundaries, which reach to the Ural Mountains. When we speak of Europe now, we mean free western Europe. The territory east of the "iron curtain," or at least a large part of it, has become so closely integrated into the Soviet system that it can no longer lay claim to many of the cultural values that we associate with the term "European."

This shrinkage in size helps to explain Europe's declining influence. Western Europe comprises only about one-fourth of the whole continent and slightly more than one-third of the area of the United States. Upon this highly civilized region, two world wars have left their deep marks. But the effect of these wars has not been quite so disastrous and lasting as one might have expected. Western Europe's more than three hundred million people, her wealth of raw materials, and her highly developed industries still leave her the most valuable region for its size in the world. Western Europe today produces almost as much coal and steel as the United States and still outproduces the Soviet Union. We must, therefore, not exaggerate the decline of European influence. It has been a relative decline, as Russia and the United States have assumed the determining roles in world affairs. But as a potential "third force" in the global balance of power, Europe, at least for the present, remains far more important than the underdeveloped regions of Asia and Africa that have so recently become emancipated from European control.

The postwar problems facing the nations of free Europe differed in each case. There were few territorial or political changes, except in Germany and Italy. The threat of communism was greater in some countries, notably France and Italy, than in others. The one need confronting all the powers, big and small, was to recover from the economic effects of the war and to regain the place that they had held in the world economy before the war. The governments differed in the methods they employed to bring about economic recovery, ranging from the socialist measures of Britain's Labor government to the free-enterprise economy of the German Federal Republic. In their efforts to find a solution to their economic troubles, the nations of western Europe were brought face to face with the necessity of modifying their traditional nationalism in the direction of some form of European union. As we shall see, this movement toward integration has gone only part of the way. For the time being, the history of

Europe continues to be the history of its major powers, Great Britain, France, Germany, and Italy.

GREAT BRITAIN— EUROPEAN OR WORLD POWER?

It took Great Britain almost a decade to recover from the effects of World War II. She had fought longer than any other power against the Axis and had suffered heavy losses. But the chief problem facing the British government was a perennial one, dating back before the war: How to support more than fifty million people on an area only slightly larger than New England, poor in natural resources and dependent on foreign imports for most of its food. In the past Britain had met this challenge through income from foreign investments and merchant shipping, and through exports of industrial goods. But the costs of war had drastically reduced Britain's foreign holdings; the loss of half her merchant tonnage reduced her carrying trade; and her exports amounted to only 30 per cent of what they had been before the war. Britain's major efforts clearly had to be concentrated upon regaining her economic health.

In July, 1945, the British people, for the first time in ten years, went to the polls. Despite the valiant wartime leadership of Winston Churchill, his Conservative Party was defeated and the coalition government replaced by a Labor government headed by Clement R. Attlee. The Labor Party advocated far-reaching socialization to solve Britain's economic ills. Between 1946 and 1948 Parliament extended the already existing social insurance system by such measures as the Education Act and the National Health Service Act. During the same period several key industries and utilities were put under public ownership; and a bill passed in 1949 called for the nationalization of the iron and steel industries by 1951. Taken as a whole, the socialization measures of the Labor government affected only some 20 per cent of Britain's industry. Yet their effects, felt in almost every sphere of British life, amounted to nothing less than a social and economic revolution.

To help overcome Britain's immediate economic difficulties, however, socialization, in the opinion of the Conservative opposition at least, was a hindrance rather than a help. To solve the basic problem of achieving a positive balance of exports over imports, a number of other measures were tried. The United States, by direct loans and through the Marshall Plan, did its share to help. The British public, meanwhile, was subjected to an austerity program of continued rationing, long working hours, and heavy taxation. In August, 1949, the British government devalued the pound from $4.03 to $2.80, in the hope that lower prices would mean increased exports. As a result of these various efforts, Britain's economy began to show marked improvement. But this trend was interrupted by the Korean war, which raised the cost of raw materials on the world market and thus helped to undo much of Britain's earlier progress.

The slowness of Britain's economic recovery, though due chiefly to causes beyond anyone's control, was blamed on the Labor government. The disappointment of the public with the party they had swept into office in 1945 was reflected in the outcome of the elections in 1951, which returned a Conservative majority. But the change in government did not bring the complete reversal of Labor's radical innovations that many people had expected. The only major socialist measure that was repealed was the projected nationalization of the steel industry. Beginning in 1952 things definitely began looking up. Government controls were removed, taxes were cut, and rationing was gradually abolished. In June, 1953, Britain and her friends celebrated the coronation of Queen Elizabeth II, who had succeeded George VI upon his death the year before. There were occasional checks in the recovery caused by major strikes. Yet with production booming, with a merchant fleet second only to that of the United States, and with ambitious building programs, the country, after ten years of hard work, seemed to have regained its economic equilibrium. In April, 1955, Sir Winston Churchill, now in his eighty-first year, resigned as prime minister and was succeeded by Sir Anthony Eden. The same year the electorate expressed its satisfaction with the way things were going by returning an increased Conservative majority to the House of Commons.

Britain was temporarily diverted from domestic issues by the government's intervention in the Suez crisis in the fall of 1956 (see p. 164). But except for causing the resignation of Prime Minister Eden, who was succeeded by Harold Macmillan, the events in Egypt had no lasting effect at home. On the contrary, when the time for another election came in 1959, the Conservatives won an even larger victory. The government's pledge that it would double the British standard of living within one generation seemed borne out by the greater abundance of consumer goods. The Labor Party, since 1955 under the leadership of Hugh Gaitskell, had nothing to match these Conservative achievements, and Labor's program of further socialization apparently held little appeal for the British voter. Nor did the majority of the British people favor a more neutralist course in foreign policy, as advocated by a radical group within the Labor Party.

The hopes aroused by the Conservative victory, however, were only partly fulfilled. Prosperity continued, but so did unemployment. There were those who doubted the soundness of Britain's economy, pointing to its slow rate of growth and lagging productivity compared with other nations. Other critics felt that much still needed to be done to assure that the nation's wealth was shared more widely through better wages and pensions, improved education, public housing, and other measures of social improvement. Further cause for alarm was seen in the sharp increase in the crime rate and in the series of scandals involving persons in high places. Reversals in foreign policy added fuel to the mounting criticism of the government and in October, 1963, led to the resignation of the ailing Macmillan. His successor, the Earl of Home, or Sir Alec Douglas-Home, as he became known after renouncing his peerage, belonged to the conservative wing of his party. The Labor opposition, meanwhile, had chosen Harold Wilson to succeed Hugh Gaitskell, who had died unexpectedly in January, 1963. A highly skilled politician, Wilson worked hard to unite his party and to give it a more moderate public image. The showdown between Labor and Conservatives came in the fall elections of 1964. Despite growing dissatisfaction with Conservative rule, the results were very close. Labor won a majority of only four seats in Parliament, which was too narrow to allow for any sweeping changes in Britain's policy. Her new prime minister, Harold Wilson, nevertheless announced that his government would tackle resolutely the many serious problems facing his country.

A good share of Britain's difficulties since World War II has been due to the fact that her once mighty empire has undergone a rapid and radical shrinkage. Wherever after 1945 colonial peoples became restive and demanded concessions or independence, British interests were involved. From India, Burma, and Malaya to Egypt, the Suez Canal, and Cyprus, Britain either was defeated or found herself on the defensive. Most of the newly independent native

43

states, however, did not completely sever their ties with Great Britain. Instead they joined the United Kingdom and her older Dominions—Canada, Australia, New Zealand, and South Africa—in that elusive organization of autonomous states known since 1948 as the "Commonwealth of Nations" (without the former designation of "British"). Since 1945 more than fifteen new nations have become members of the Commonwealth: India, Pakistan, Ceylon, Ghana, Nigeria, Cyprus, Sierra Leone, Tanzania (Tanganyika and Zanzibar), Jamaica, Trinidad and Tobago, Uganda, Malaysia, Kenya, Malawi (Nyasaland), Malta, and Zambia (Northern Rhodesia). Others—Burma and the Sudan—became members for a short time only. Two of the older members, Ireland and South Africa, also have left the Commonwealth. Some of the new members, like India, Pakistan, and Ghana, are republics and thus recognize the British sovereign merely as "Head of the Commonwealth." The size of the Commonwealth, with more than a quarter of the world's surface and population, is impressive. But in order to survive, this loose federation has to justify its usefulness, which now is chiefly economic. The majority of Commonwealth people today are nonwhite and as such highly critical of the colonialism which their former mother country exercises in what is left of the British Empire. Great Britain, on the other hand, hopes to maintain and enlarge the Commonwealth. Together with her few remaining overseas possessions, the Commonwealth association provides Britain with the appearance at least of being still a world power.

It is understandable, in view of her great past, that Britain should want to continue playing a leading role in world affairs. For this reason she has remained cool toward any projects for closer economic or political integration among western European states, unless her special position within the Commonwealth is taken into account (see p. 63). It remains to be seen how long Britain can afford to remain aloof from the continent. In the military field she has already broken precedent by entering into a series of peacetime continental alliances. Economic necessity may force Britain into still closer alignment with western Europe, even though she may thus incur the displeasure of her Commonwealth associates.

More important than either her collaboration with the Commonwealth or with western Europe are England's relations with the United States. These, by necessity, have been very close, although not always too cordial. Britain at times has resented her dependence upon the United States and on occasion—as in her recognition of Red China and her trade with Cuba—has followed an independent course. The Suez crisis of 1956 cast a deep, though passing, shadow on Anglo-American relations (see p. 164). Since then the major source of friction between the two has come from England's role as a nuclear power. In the fall of 1956 the Royal Air Force tested Britain's first atomic bomb and by May, 1957, Britain had developed her own H-bomb. When it came to delivering these nuclear weapons by way of ballistic missiles, however, Britain found the going too expensive. Instead she depended upon the United States to supply her with a new type of missile, the Skybolt. In 1962 America suddenly decided to abandon the Skybolt. The announcement to this effect was greeted in England by a wave of anti-American criticism. British feelings were only partly healed by the Nassau agreement between President Kennedy and Prime Minister Macmillan in December, 1962, which substituted Polaris for Skybolt missiles. Yet despite these and other differences, there can be no doubt about the "special relationship" between Great Britain and the United States and their common interest in the strengthening of the Atlantic community.

FRANCE—THE QUEST FOR LOST GRANDEUR

France, like Great Britain, suffered acutely from problems of postwar economic readjustment. But, unlike Britain, France's efforts at recovery were seriously hampered by political instability. The French political picture at the end of the war looked encouraging. After the liberation in 1944 a provisional government was formed by merging the wartime Committee of National Liberation with various resistance groups. This new regime was headed by General Charles de Gaulle, hero of the Free French Movement. It was chiefly under De Gaulle's direction that the transition from the Vichy regime of the past to the future Fourth Republic was accomplished. The most urgent tasks of the provisional government were economic. Under pressure from its leftist members, the government in 1945 embarked on a program of extensive nationalization of key industries. Simultaneously a planning council, under the brilliant economist Jean Monnet, worked out a blueprint for

French recovery. It was at this critical point that the confusion of French politics intervened.

As a result of the elections for a National Constituent Assembly in October, 1945, more than three-quarters of the seats were almost equally divided among the Socialists, the Communists, and the Popular Republicans, a new party advocating moderate social reform. The Communists received the largest single vote. In January, 1946, General de Gaulle, who had found cooperation with the leftists increasingly difficult, resigned the provisional presidency. In October a new constitution was adopted. It closely resembled that of the Third Republic, with an all-powerful National Assembly, a primarily consultative Council of the Republic (the former Senate), and a weak executive.

The root of France's difficulties under the Fourth Republic, as under the Third, continued to be the innumerable divisions among its electorate, resulting in a multiplicity of parties and making the formation of viable coalition governments practically impossible. In the course of ten years the Fourth Republic had more than twenty cabinets, lasting anywhere from a few days to slightly over a year. Until May, 1947, a leftist majority kept matters relatively stable, but from then on confusion again became the order of the day. In April, 1947, General de Gaulle re-entered the political arena with a new party, the Reunion of the French People. Its purpose was to serve as a counterweight to the Communists. The parties between these two extremes tried to steer a middle course. Yet they found it difficult to agree on the continuation or abolition of social reforms and nationalization. If France somehow managed to continue functioning despite incessant domestic crises, this was due to her centralized bureaucracy and excellent system of municipal government, as well as to the fact that a number of unusually able men—Robert Schuman, René Pleven, Jules Moch, René Mayer, and others—served in different positions under various cabinets, thus insuring a certain continuity of policy.

The instability of France's domestic affairs was enhanced by the serious problems she faced abroad. The basic element of French foreign policy during the first years after the war was its dependence on American support, a relationship that was obnoxious to French pride. To regain some measure of initiative in foreign affairs, the French in the spring of 1950 became the chief advocates of a program of European union (see p. 61 ff.). But such a policy immediately raised a question on which most Frenchmen had very strong feelings—the future of Franco-German relations. Events elsewhere, especially in Korea, hastened the integration of Germany into the Western camp. But France found it difficult at first to admit her recent enemy into a partnership that might some day become German-dominated.

One of the problems which France shared with Great Britain concerned the future of the French colonial empire, the second largest in the world. To counteract the disruptive effects of native unrest, the constitution of the Fourth Republic called for the establishment of the French Union, consisting of the mother country and its overseas territories. It was headed by the president of the Republic and a High Council made up of representatives of the Union's members. The purpose of the Union was to preserve France's empire through greater administrative centralization. In this respect the French Union differed from Britain's Commonwealth with its emphasis on decentralization. Since France's overseas possessions demanded a greater degree of independence, the French Union was not very effective. Like Great Britain, France was plagued by almost continuous nationalist revolts in her colonies, notably in Indochina and in North Africa. The war in Indochina, which lasted until 1954, cost France more than thirty-five thousand lives and more than twice the amount of money she had received under the Marshall Plan. Despite these sacrifices, part of Indochina was lost to the Communist world, and the rest of France's former dependencies—Laos, Cambodia, and South Vietnam—after a brief stay in the French Union, declared their independence (see p. 156). A similar fate overtook most of France's holdings in the Middle East and in North Africa. The only territory where she decided to stand firm was Algeria, France's oldest possession in North Africa and part of Metropolitan France. It was the continued unrest in Algeria that led to the French crisis of 1958 which ended the Fourth Republic.

In view of France's political problems at home and abroad, it is not surprising that her economic recovery was extremely slow. French financial burdens after World War II were staggering. There were the costs of the war itself, not only for the repair of war damage, but also for pensions and annuities. Then there was the continued financial drain from the fighting in Indochina and the contribution to European rearmament. Added to these military expenses were the costs of the new social security system. And finally, in order to compete successfully on the world market, French industry required vast sums for the replacement of outmoded equipment and improvement of inefficient production methods. To meet these manifold obligations a strict system of taxation and a sound currency were needed. Efforts to reform the tax structure met with the traditional opposition of the French taxpayer, and the creeping inflation of the franc served to discourage saving and investment. Economic aid, chiefly under the Marshall Plan, did much to improve France's economy, and by 1949 the prewar level of industrial production had been regained. But by the middle of 1950 the trading crisis caused by the Korean war, the intensification of the war in Indochina, and the increased need for defense spending in Europe combined to undo much of the earlier progress. The situation was made still worse by an almost uninterrupted series of strikes, most of them led by the pro-Communist General Federation of Labor (CGT).

It was only after 1953 that the French economic picture began to brighten. Every possible method was tried to aid recovery—price control, reduction of government spending, curtailment of imports, export subsidies, public works, tax reform, building loans, and currency devaluation. By 1958 these combined efforts had resulted in a noticeable improvement. But the French economy was still far from sound. Much of the recovery had been due to continued foreign aid, principally from the United States. And what changes for the better there were had been won only against the bitter resistance of the many interest groups entrenched in the National Assembly. Here was the basic cause of France's troubles: the tenacity with which the French people clung to their individual, group, and regional interests, suspicious of concentrated political power and averse to any purposeful direction of national affairs. The resulting political instability not only retarded economic development, it also prevented the solution of France's most burning political problem: the future of Algeria.

Fighting in Algeria between an Arab independence movement led by the National Liberation Front and the French army had been going on since 1954. By 1958 it had cost the lives of five thousand Frenchmen and fifty thousand Algerians. Efforts to reach a compromise were fought by right-wing groups in Paris and by the more than one million persons of French extraction in Algeria. It was over rumors of another such compromise in May, 1958, that the colonists staged a riot in Algiers. They were joined by army units, embittered over France's previous futile colonial campaigns and over the government's indecisiveness. A "Committee of Public Safety" called on General de Gaulle to form a French government "capable of restoring the grandeur and independence of the mother land." To avoid the outbreak of civil war, the government and De Gaulle collaborated on a legal and orderly transfer of power. On June 1, 1958, De Gaulle was made premier with full power to revise the constitution. In September the new constitution of the Fifth Republic was adopted by popular referendum. Its outstanding characteristic was the increased power it gave to the president. In December, 1958, General de Gaulle was elected president of the republic. He took office on January 8, 1959.

Since then the French political scene has been dominated by the towering figure of Charles de Gaulle. His powers and functions are similar to those of the American chief executive. He has used these powers to gain stability at home and to increase French prestige abroad. The National Assembly, shorn of its arbitrary powers and with a majority of Gaullist supporters, passed a broad austerity program that imposed sacrifices upon each and every Frenchman. Such sacrifices were needed, according to De Gaulle, to rescue France from economic stagnation and to make her once again a self-sustaining nation. Only a France thus strengthened could support her claim to "grandeur" in the international sphere. De Gaulle's economic measures took some time to make themselves felt. Meanwhile rapidly rising prices led to frequent strikes among workers and demonstrations among farmers. While the Algerian war continued, military expenses and the influx of Algerian refugees put a heavy burden on the treasury. But the careful planning characteristic of France's economy since World War II was beginning to bear fruit. While prices rose, so did wages. The gross national product kept increasing by more than 5 per cent annually; unemployment was minimal; and large gold and dollar reserves testified to the basic soundness of the French economy. The French people's satisfaction with De Gaulle's leadership was shown in the support they gave him in various referendums and in the national elections of November, 1962. The latter brought a resounding victory to the Gaullist forces, notably the Union for the New Republic (UNR). In October, 1962, the voters approved a constitutional amendment providing for popular, rather than indirect, election of future presidents. This was a further victory for De Gaulle's concept of presidential government.

The most important achievement of De Gaulle has been his

solution of the Algerian problem. In September, 1959, he announced that lasting peace could be won only on the basis of self-
determination. This proposal aroused violent protests among
rightists at home and French settlers and the army in Algeria.
But the majority of Frenchmen applauded the prospect of ending a costly and "dirty" war. Negotiations for a cease-fire were
begun in the summer of 1960, but agreement was not reached
until 1962. A revolt led by French officers in Algeria in 1961 was
put down, but the Secret Army Organization (OAS) continued
its atrocities and extended its terrorist activities to France, where
several attempts were made on De Gaulle's life. On March 17
French and Arab representatives finally signed the agreement at
Evian-les-Bains that gave Algeria her independence. It received
overwhelming popular endorsement except by the white settlers
in Algeria.

Next to solving the Algerian question, De Gaulle's major concern has been with reasserting French power and influence abroad.
In doing so, he has frequently taken an independent and intransi-
gent stand on important issues, a fact that has not endeared him
to his friends and allies. He has withdrawn the French Mediterranean fleet from NATO control; he has insisted upon an independent nuclear policy for France; he has opposed the formation
of a multinational NATO nuclear force; and he has vetoed Britain's
entry into the European Economic Community. The French
people have warmly supported this show of independence. To
strengthen France's position further, De Gaulle has cooperated
closely with West Germany. Overseas he has helped transform
the former French Union into the present French Community.
As constituted in 1958, the Community consists of the French
Republic, its few remaining overseas possessions (mostly in the
Caribbean), and some of the new African states that formerly
made up French Equatorial and French West Africa. It is a loose
and informal federation, more important for the prestige than for
any practical advantages it offers. But then, prestige is an important word in De Gaulle's vocabulary. His aim is to recapture
some of the grandeur that once was France's, to place his country
at the head of a European confederation, and to join the two
Anglo-Saxon powers in the leadership of the free world. This program may seem unrealistic and impossible of attainment, but that
does not seem to faze *le grand Charles*.

WEST GERMANY—
THE "ECONOMIC MIRACLE"

We have already seen how the division of Germany came about in the course of the cold war. Today the Federal Republic of Germany is recognized by the West as the only legitimate German government. The so-called German Democratic Republic in the east is merely another Russian satellite and in Western eyes is still regarded as the Soviet zone of occupation. The Federal Republic is by far the more important of the two Germanies. It is more than twice the size and has three times the population of East Germany, and it produces more than fifty times as much coal and almost ten times as much steel.

Of all the major powers of Europe, West Germany has shown the most spectacular rise from rubble to riches. The key event that set this recovery in motion was the reform of West Germany's currency in 1948. The establishment of the sound and solid *Deutsche Mark* revived the Germans' confidence in their country's future and thus helped to unleash the tremendous energy characteristic of that disciplined and industrious people. The "economic miracle," therefore, was due first and foremost to the efficiency and hard work of the Germans. But Germany's recovery would have been impossible without material and technical aid from the West, particularly from the United States.

The economic problems faced by Germany as a result of the war were overwhelming. Destruction from Allied bombing was not as serious as had been expected. But the postwar dismantling of factories and the separation of the western industrial from the eastern agricultural regions made economic revival seem quite hopeless. The influx of some nine (ultimately thirteen) million refugees and expellees into the already crowded west, the lack of essential raw materials except coal, and the severance of all international economic relations further aggravated the situation. The first three years after the war until 1948 were chiefly devoted to keeping the German people from starving. In this task American aid proved decisive. On the eve of the currency reform in 1948 the German index of production was only slightly more than 40 per cent of its 1936 level. More than two million Germans were unemployed. Exports, the only hope for economic survival, were at a mere trickle.

Then the "economic miracle" happened. The direction of Germany's reconstruction was in the hands of Minister of Economics Dr. Ludwig Erhard. He was a firm believer in a "free-market economy," that is, free enterprise at home and free trade abroad. This approach, fundamentally different from the nationalization policies of France and Great Britain, turned out to be a great success. Germany's industrial output by 1950 had regained its 1936 level and by 1957 it had more than doubled. In 1962 the gross national product was close to 85 billion dollars; Germany's foreign trade at the same time exceeded 25 billion dollars; and real wages were almost double what they had been before the war. With a favorable trade balance, Germany was able to build up a sizeable reserve of gold and foreign currency, some of which has been used since 1960 for foreign aid. There is virtually no unemployment in West Germany; on the contrary, there is a shortage of labor, necessitating the employment of some eight hundred fifty thousand foreign workers.

It is quite fitting that in dealing with postwar Germany we should begin by discussing her economic recovery, since this was her major problem and achievement. But it is doubtful if this recovery would have proceeded so smoothly if it had not been for the political stability of the new republic. This stability was largely due to the firm and able leadership of Germany's first chancellor, Konrad Adenauer. The Federal Republic, with Bonn as its capital, came into existence in May, 1949. Its constitution called for a legislature of two houses, the *Bundestag* and the *Bundesrat*. The *Bundestag* is elected by universal suffrage on the basis of proportional representation. The *Bundesrat* is appointed by, and represents, the governments of the various federal states. Executive power is vested in a strong chancellor. The president, as head of state, performs mainly ceremonial functions. The first elections in August, 1949, pretty well set the political pattern that has existed since. Adenauer's middle-of-the-road Christian Democratic Union (CDU) received the largest number of votes. But to form a workable government, the CDU had to enter into a coalition with the right-wing liberal Free Democratic Party (FDP). The opposition has been led by the Social Democratic Party (SPD). Until his death in 1952 the SPD was led by the dynamic Kurt Schumacher. He was succeeded by Erich Ollenhauer, who died in 1963. Since early 1964 the popular and personable mayor of West Berlin, Willy Brandt, has been chairman of the SPD.

The Socialists command the second largest number of votes, and their program, after relinquishing its Marxist dogmatism and anti-clericalism, appeals to a growing number of voters. There were some smaller parties at first, but the trend in recent years has been in the direction of a two-party system. Communist strength in West Germany has been negligible, especially since the Communist Party was outlawed in 1956. A similar fate befell the neo-Nazi German Reichs Party, which never gained more than 1.2 per cent of the popular vote.

Aside from economic questions, the two most important issues before the West German government have been reunification and rearmament. The first of these has been on the agenda of most major conferences between the East and West since 1949, but the powers have been unable to reach any agreement. The insistence of the Western powers on free general elections as the only peaceful method of achieving German unity has run into consistent Soviet opposition, since such elections would doubtless spell the end of communism in East Germany. The problem of reunification became more complicated as Germany in 1952 prepared to join the defensive alliance of the West. Russia asserted that such a step would make reunification impossible. The majority of Germans followed Chancellor Adenauer in his undeviating adherance to the Western line, sharing the chancellor's belief that a strong West was the best guarantee for ultimate reunification. But there was also a strong minority, centered in the Social Democrats, which advocated a neutralist position for Germany to facilitate negotiations with the Russians. As the fruitlessness of such negotiations became obvious, however, the Socialist opposition relented in its criticism of Adenauer's policy and finally, in 1960, officially accepted the Western alliance.

While German reunification has remained an unfulfilled hope, West German rearmament has made considerable progress. The initial aim of the victorious powers had been the complete disarmament and demilitarization of Germany. The Germans, with the memory of the war fresh in their minds, found little fault with such a policy and included a provision in their new constitution forbidding conscription and outlawing a German national army. But as the threat of Communist aggression in Europe increased, as Russia began training a German military force in East Germany, and as war broke out in Korea, the Western powers thought it desirable to have Germany participate in the security system of the West. German rearmament took five years, from 1950 to 1955, to get under way. To overcome the fears of the French against the revival of German militarism, Germany's contribution to Western defense was first envisaged within the framework of a supranational European Defense Community (EDC). The necessary agreements for EDC were signed in 1952. But French apprehension of Germany continued to be too strong, and the French National Assembly refused to ratify the EDC treaty. As a substitute the British then proposed a revision of the Brussels Treaty of 1948 so as to include Germany in the Western European Union and in NATO. Final agreement on this plan was reached at Paris in October, 1954, and ratified by the French Assembly the following December.

But opposition to German rearmament was not restricted to the French. There also were strong forces in Germany who, from genuine pacifism or from a desire for neutralism, tried to block the constitutional amendments necessary to make Germany part of NATO. Due to the skill and perseverance of Chancellor Adenauer, these obstacles were gradually overcome, and the Paris treaties of October, 1954, were finally ratified by Germany on May 5, 1955. Under the provisions of these treaties, Germany was to have an armed force of 500,000 men. This figure was later modified to 350,000. Germany renounced the right to produce atomic, biological, or chemical weapons as well as long-distance guided missiles. She also agreed to inspection of her armament industries by the Western powers. In return for assuming these obligations, West Germany regained her full sovereignty under the Paris treaties. The only remaining restriction gives the three former occupying powers the right to keep their military forces on German soil.

Even though West Germany did not regain her full independence until May 5, 1955, she had for several years been conducting a quite independent foreign policy. Both by necessity and by conviction that policy had been immutable in its support of the West. The Germans did not share any of the overseas difficulties of the French and British, since Germany had lost her colonial empire after World War I. Closer to home, plans for some kind of European union found the warmest support in West Germany, especially among the young. The constitution of the Federal Republic specifically permits the German government to yield its sovereignty to such a union, should it ever become a reality. Any such scheme, however, depends first and foremost on good rela-

tions between France and Germany. The attainment of such relations remained one of Chancellor Adenauer's major goals.

The beginnings of the rapprochement between France and
West Germany go back to the early 1950's, when the two nations
decided to bury their "hereditary enmity" and to collaborate in
the economic unification of western Europe (see p. 62). For a
while disagreement over the Saar, a coal-rich region on the Franco-
German border, kept the two nations apart. The French after
World War II had attached the area to France, hoping to gain a
permanent hold over it. But since most of the Saar's inhabitants
were German, this policy did not work. In 1955 the majority of
the population voted to return to Germany. The political reunion
with the Federal Republic came about in 1957, and the economic
transfer was effected in 1959. Since then collaboration between
France and West Germany has been close, both economically and
politically. On January 22, 1963, the two powers signed a treaty of
friendship which calls for periodic meetings between their heads
of state and leading officials. Relations between the two grand old
men, Adenauer and De Gaulle, in the last few years clearly indi-
cated that their friendship was real.

Germany's close contacts with France could not but involve her in some of De Gaulle's squabbles with his Anglo-Saxon
allies. Adenauer's relations with Great Britain, while correct, had
never been cordial. At times he suspected the British of being soft
toward the Russians. Relations with the United States during the
Eisenhower-Dulles era had been intimate, but they became less
so under Kennedy. America's failure to take a firmer stand against
the building of the Berlin wall, her signing of the test ban treaty,
and her wheat sales to Russia all came in for heavy criticism from
Adenauer. Yet Adenauer's distrust of the "Anglo-Saxons" was
largely a personal matter and did not affect Germany's stand on
such vital issues as participation in the multilateral atomic force
of NATO or Britain's admission to the Common Market, both of
which West Germany supported, despite De Gaulle's objections.
The retirement of Adenauer from the chancellorship on October
15, 1963, furthermore, brought to an end the "Adenauer era" and
ushered in a new phase in Germany's relations with the West.

The chancellor's retirement had been predicted for some time,
yet he had managed to hold on to the power he loved so well.
Adenauer's strong and authoritarian personality had discouraged
the rise of possible rivals who might have succeeded him. The new

chancellor, Ludwig Erhard, certainly does not exude his predecessor's air of authority and statesmanship. But as the architect of West Germany's economic recovery, he commands the respect and affection of his countrymen. His domestic achievements in the past speak for themselves and hardly need to be improved upon. In his foreign policy Erhard depends less on friendly relations with France than Adenauer had done, and instead, recognizes the need for closer partnership between western Europe and the United States in the Atlantic community.

The pro-Western and democratic policy of the West German government is generally taken as proof that the Germans have made a sincere break with their recent Nazi past. There have been few incidents of neo-Nazism, and in recent years a number of Nazi criminals, who had escaped trial before, were finally brought to justice. Yet there has been little feeling of responsibility among individual Germans for the horrible deeds their nation committed during the Nazi years; nor has there been more than perfunctory recognition of the generosity that the Western powers have shown in helping Germany get back on her feet. In their feverish preoccupation with material concerns, the Germans show little of the give-and-take in their dealings with each other and with outsiders that is part of the democratic way of life. The government and a highly responsible press are trying to educate the German people in the ways of democracy; but this is a slow process. It will take time and continued peace and prosperity before the effects of these efforts at self-education can be felt.

ITALY—POVERTY IN THE MIDST OF PLENTY

In a world where major decisions are reserved for superpowers and where the traditional great powers are relegated to secondary positions, the weight of the smaller nations counts for very little. Even a country like Italy, in the past a member of the major league, today is no longer in the same class with Britain, France, or West Germany. Heavily overpopulated, short of capital and basic raw materials, and without enough good soil to produce sufficient food, Italy was slow to recover from the effects of World War II, which had left her already backward economy in a dismal state. Yet despite these handicaps the Italians, through hard work and with generous foreign aid, have been able to perform their own economic miracle. After a slow start Italy's economy in the late fifties and early sixties showed the highest rate of economic growth in the West. Her adverse balance of trade and payments has been reversed, foreign capital is moving into the country at a fast pace, and the standard of living of most Italians has improved visibly. Growing prosperity, furthermore, has brought a drop in the birth rate which will help alleviate population pressure.

Yet the picture is not all rosy. While there is prosperity, there is also still much poverty; and while there is a boom, there is also still much unemployment. Most of the progress has been in the industrial north. There have been far fewer improvements in the agricultural south. The government has tried to bridge this gap between the two regions by introducing land reform and industry into the south, but much still remains to be done. Even in the north real wages have not kept up with the general rise in the economy, and the distribution of income remains quite uneven. There is need for additional schools, more social services, stricter enforcement of tax laws, and a general clean-up of the bureaucracy. The fact that one out of every four Italians voted Communist in the 1963 elections shows that all is far from well with the Italian economic and social system.

Popular discontent has been reflected in political instability. The Italian political scene since World War II has been noted for its incessant political crises. In June, 1946, a popular referendum abolished the monarchy and established a republic. For a while the chief anti-Fascist parties—Christian Democrats, Socialists, and Communists—collaborated under the leadership of Alcide de Gasperi to insure a certain degree of stability. But with the coming of the cold war this cooperation came to an end. In the crucial elections of 1948 communism was the main issue. De Gasperi's Christian Democrats received a majority, but the Communists, under their veteran leader Palmiro Togliatti, emerged as the second largest party. Together with the left wing of the Socialists, under Pietro Nenni, the Communists embarked on a vigorous campaign of obstructing Italy's alignment with the West. Communist domination of Italy's largest labor union, the General Confederation of Labor, led to an uninterrupted series of strikes. On the extreme right a neo-Fascist party, the Italian Social Movement, while never becoming a real threat, added further to the general instability. The gradual drift from center to left continued in the elections of

57

1953, which brought the Christian Democrats and their allies a very slim majority and gave more than a third of the popular vote to the left. The strength of the left increased further in the 1958 and 1963 elections. The Christian Democrats, while remaining the largest group, needed outside support to be able to form a viable government. This they found among the parties of the moderate left (Republicans and Democratic Socialists) or the moderate right (Liberals). Since 1962 the trend to the left has predominated. At that time the government invited the support of the left-wing Socialists, who had hitherto cooperated with the Communists. This "opening to the left" continued after the 1963 elections when the Socialists temporarily joined the government. The Communists, meanwhile, tried to renew their "unity of action" pact with the Socialists, hoping to force Italy into a more radical course at home and a neutralist course abroad.

Despite neutralist sentiment among many Italians, the government has been undeviating in its support of the West. Italy was among the founders of NATO and of the Common Market, and she was admitted to the United Nations in 1955. On all major issues of the cold war she has sided with the United States and Great Britain. We have already noted Italy's disappointment over the peace settlement of 1947. The problem of Trieste, which had remained unsettled at that time, was solved in 1954 by the partition of the region between Italy and Yugoslavia. In her role as a former colonial power Italy has tried to mediate between the Western and Arab powers in the Middle East. Her resentment over the loss of her own colonies has subsided, as native nationalism almost everywhere has put an end to colonialism.

THE SMALL NATIONS OF WESTERN EUROPE

Next to Italy the most important among the smaller powers of western Europe are the three "Benelux" countries—Belgium, the Netherlands, and Luxembourg. All three of them are constitutional monarchies. Belgium changed rulers in 1951 when King Leopold III, unpopular because of his surrender to the Germans and his marriage to a commoner, abdicated in favor of his eldest son, King Baudouin I. In the Netherlands Queen Juliana succeeded her mother, Queen Wilhelmina, in 1948; and in Luxembourg Prince Jean succeeded Grand Duchess Charlotte in 1964. Political leadership in all three countries is exercised by Catholic and Socialist parties that, on the whole, have worked together successfully. Both Belgium and Luxembourg, after a brief period of transition, soon regained their prewar prosperity, while it took Holland several years to regain her economic balance. The three nations are quite dependent on economic exchange with France and particularly Germany, and have played a leading role in the economic integration of western Europe. As a first step they formed the Benelux Union in 1948, which established a customs union among its three members. Both Belgium and Holland still had extensive colonial empires at the end of the war, but except for a few Dutch islands in the Caribbean, these have now been lost. In their foreign relations the Benelux countries have been firmly in the Western camp.

In discussing some of the remaining small powers of western Europe we can be brief. Spain had managed to stay out of World War II, but her benevolent neutrality toward Hitler and the repressive regime of Fascist dictator Francisco Franco left her an outcast among the democratic nations of the West. These nations, together with Russia, refused to admit Spain to the United Nations when that organization was founded. With the coming of the cold war, however, the strategic importance of the Iberian peninsula somewhat modified Western coldness. Opposition to Spain remained strong enough to prevent her participation in the Marshall Plan and in NATO. Instead, the United States and Spain in 1953 concluded a bilateral agreement that permitted American use of Spanish air and naval bases in return for economic aid. The agreement was renewed for five years in 1963. Spain won a further diplomatic victory in 1955, when she was at long last admitted to the United Nations. Portugal, which was admitted at the same time, has been under a similar cloud because of the authoritarian regime of Premier Oliveira Salazar. Her readiness to permit Allied use of the Azores as an air base during World War II, however, and her long-standing alliance with Great Britain have made Portugal somewhat more acceptable to the West. This acceptance was evidenced by her participation in the founding of NATO. Both Spain and Portugal still have African colonies. While Spain's negligible holdings have been granted partial autonomy, Portugal's sizeable possessions in Angola and Mozambique are considered part of the mother country, which has refused to give way to pressure from the free African nations that Portugal grant independence to her "overseas provinces."

The three Scandinavian countries—Denmark, Sweden, and

Norway—are constitutional monarchies with ruling houses that enjoy considerable popularity. Denmark suffered less than any other country from German occupation. Sweden, because of her neutrality, actually prospered during the war. The Scandinavian nations have made satisfactory economic recovery and, like the Benelux countries, have moved toward closer economic integration. All three are members of the European Free Trade Association. Sweden continues in her traditional policy of neutrality, maintaining close, though not always very satisfactory, economic relations with the Soviet Union. Both Denmark and Norway, on the other hand, have from the very beginnings of NATO placed their forces behind that defensive alliance of the West. Premier Khrushchev, during a state visit to the Scandinavian countries in 1964, found the people friendly but distant.

The small republic of Austria, finally, is in a category by itself. Although considered a "liberated" rather than a defeated country, Austria was placed under four-power occupation in 1945. The Western Allies did everything they could to aid Austria's recovery; but their efforts were nullified by the Russians, who insisted on payment of large reparations. The Austrian government was eager for a final peace settlement, and the Austrian question was discussed at every East-West conference. For ten years after the war Austria remained one of the major issues in the cold war. It was not until 1955 that the Soviet Union relented in its obstructionist attitude and it was possible to make peace. The Austrian State Treaty of May 15, 1955, recognized the independence of Austria and prohibited any future *Anschluss* (union) with Germany. Occupation troops were withdrawn in October, 1955, and two months later Austria was admitted to the United Nations. Russia's good will had to be bought at the price of large financial compensations as well as an Austrian promise of strict neutrality between East and West. But Austria's sympathies, like those of neutral Switzerland, are firmly with the West. Austria's economic recovery, thanks to Western aid, has been remarkable, and she enjoys a stable prosperity unprecedented in the history of the republic. Austria is a member of the European Free Trade Association.

THE QUEST FOR EUROPEAN UNITY

Our brief survey of recent events in western Europe clearly shows that the old continent had lost none of its traditional diversity.

In their attempts to solve their postwar difficulties most of its nations have used widely varying solutions. Yet the difficulties themselves have shown great similarity. The need for economic recovery and the search for military security have been the foremost problems faced by each European government since 1945. It has become increasingly clear that neither problem is capable of unilateral solution. If Europe is to survive and play an important role in world affairs, she will have to overcome her national antagonisms and work toward some form of European integration. For the first time in European history efforts have been under way since World War II to create a united Europe, not from above by force of conquest, but from below, through voluntary collaboration among the different members of the European family.

The need for collaboration was first felt in the economic field. We have already seen how the Marshall Plan helped to set up an extensive European Recovery Program under the direction of an Organization for European Economic Cooperation (OEEC). The purpose of OEEC was to promote economic recovery through cooperative action among the countries of western Europe. This step was certainly important, but it originated outside of Europe with the United States, and it failed in its prime objective: to bring about intra-European cooperation. The first sign that Europe itself understood the necessity to unite came with the Brussels Treaty of March, 1948, between Great Britain, France, and the Benelux countries. The immediate purpose of this treaty was to establish a defensive alliance against the threat of Soviet expansion; but it also called for collaboration among its members in economic, social, and cultural matters. For this purpose the treaty established a Western Union with a Council and an Assembly as governing bodies. The initial influence of this organization, however, was not very great. The Western Union was an international, rather than supranational, body, and none of its five members gave up any of their sovereign rights. Its chief military function, moreover, was gradually merged after 1949 with that of NATO. Despite its limitations, however, the Western Union opened the way for the discussion of more far-reaching projects, some of which began taking shape in the early 1950's.

The only one of these projects that materialized as originally conceived was an economic one, the famous Schuman Plan. It originated with the French economist Jean Monnet, one of the leading advocates of a united Europe. The plan was guided through its complicated negotiations by French Foreign Minister

Robert Schuman. Its main purpose was to establish a truly supra-national authority over the coal and steel industries of western Europe, insuring the free flow of these vital raw materials among the plan's six member nations—France, West Germany, Italy, and the Benelux countries. The European Coal and Steel Community (ECSC), as the organization set up under the Schuman Plan is officially called, was established by treaty on April 18, 1951, and was formally launched in 1952. ECSC has full power to fix prices, set export and import quotas, and allocate materials, unhampered by any interference on the part of a member state. It has its own governing body, the High Authority, with headquarters in the city of Luxembourg. Major policy decisions are made by the ECSC Common Assembly, elected by the parliaments of the member states. Disputes among members are settled by the Community's own Court of Justice. The ECSC is a momentous innovation. The economic interdependence of France (rich in iron ore) and Germany (rich in coal) had long been recognized. Previous efforts of France or Germany to control the whole rich industrial region, with the Rhine River as its main artery, had led to tensions and war. Some of these tensions, of course, will continue as long as there are national governments; and differences among the member states of the Community in the granting of industrial subsidies, tax structures, wage levels, and social insurance policies at first interfered with the smooth functioning of ECSC. But in time these differences were ironed out, and by 1957 the aim of a common market for coal and steel among the six nations of "Little Europe" had been achieved.

But this was only the beginning. The next steps to broaden European integration in the economic field were taken on March 25, 1957, when the members of the Coal and Steel Community signed the Rome treaties, which established the European Economic Community (EEC) or Common Market and the European Atomic Energy Community (Euratom). The moving spirit behind these new organizations again was Jean Monnet. EEC calls for the elimination of all tariff barriers among member states and the adoption of a common tariff on imports from outside the Common Market. Ultimately labor and capital as well as goods are to move freely within the European Economic Community; there is to be standardization of wages and social security systems; and there will be a common investment pool with contributions from each member state. Euratom has created an agency for the common development of atomic energy within the six-nation community, including the sharing of atomic information, joint research, and a common market for fissionable materials and equipment. Both EEC and Euratom are administered by joint institutions— an Assembly, a Council, a Commission, an Economic and Social Committee, and a Court of Justice—some of which are identical with institutions of the Coal and Steel Community.

The member nations of the European Economic Community, which includes some of the world's most highly industrialized nations and comprises a market of some 170 million customers, have been busy since 1957 making their program a reality. An investment bank and social security fund have been set up, the movement of capital inside the Common Market has been freed, and studies have been started on the free movement of labor. The most important aim of EEC, the abolition of internal tariff barriers, was originally intended to take some twelve years. But here, too, much progress has been made, and if it continues, internal tariffs will be eliminated far ahead of the 1969 target dates. The only real difficulties encountered have been with agricultural goods on which prices within member states vary widely. The move toward a common tariff against outsiders has been somewhat slower, partly because it is complicated to work out, but chiefly because it has run into considerable opposition from the European countries that are not members of EEC, as well as from the United States.

The European Economic Community is not a closed organization. Any country can apply for membership, provided it agrees to adhere to the Community's rules and policies. Greece thus became an associate member in 1962, and Turkey in 1963. A number of other countries have also applied for admission, most important among them Great Britain. The British initially had been cool toward EEC, fearing that its obligations might interfere with Britain's role within the Commonwealth. As a countermove, Great Britain in 1960 had launched the European Free Trade Association (EFTA), together with Austria, Switzerland, Portugal, Denmark, Norway, and Sweden. The aim of EFTA was to establish free trade among its members, but not to follow a uniform tariff policy against the outside world. As time went on, however, and the advantages of membership in the Common Market became obvious, Britain's attitude changed. After prolonged negotiations about the conditions under which Britain might combine adherence to EEC with membership in the Commonwealth, British

MEMBERSHIP IN EUROPEAN ORGANIZATIONS

	OEEC* OECD	ECSC EEC Euratom	EFTA	WEU	Council of Europe	NATO
Austria	x		x		x	
Belgium	x	x		x	x	x
Cyprus					x	
Denmark	x		x		x	x
France	x	x		x	x	x
West Germany	x	x		x	x	x
Greece	x	x**			x	x
Iceland	x				x	x
Ireland	x				x	
Italy	x	x		x	x	x
Luxembourg	x	x		x	x	x
Netherlands	x	x		x	x	x
Norway	x		x		x	x
Portugal	x		x			x
Spain	x					
Sweden	x		x		x	
Switzerland	x		x		x	
Turkey	x	x**			x	x
United Kingdom	x		x	x	x	x
Canada	x					x
United States	x					x

*In September, 1961, OEEC was replaced by the Organization for Economic Cooperation and Development (OECD), with Spain, Canada, and USA as additional members.
**Associated members.

entry into the Common Market was expected for some time in 1963. But these hopes were dashed when President de Gaulle, in January, 1963, vetoed Britain's entry. The move was part of De Gaulle's "grand design" to assert French and European independence vis à vis Britain and the United States. Coming at a time when EEC was already going through a period of strained relations with the United States, the French veto dealt a serious blow to the cause of European unity.

The United States from the beginning had taken a benevolent interest in the movement toward European unity, even to the point of making certain tariff concessions to the fledgling European

Community. To stress America's economic interdependence with western Europe, Washington in early 1961 had joined the new Organization for Economic Cooperation and Development (OECD), successor to the OEEC founded under the Marshall Plan. The purpose of OECD was to further economic growth and development and to contribute to the expansion of world trade. In 1962 the United States Congress passed the Trade Expansion Act, giving the President authority to reduce tariffs by as much as 50 per cent and to eliminate duties entirely on a wide range of goods. This farsighted measure was designed to bring about a relaxation of trade barriers, especially between the United States and the European Common Market. When it came to implementing the act, however, interest groups on both sides put up determined resistance. Attempts of the Common Market to keep American poultry out of the European market led to the "chicken war" of 1963, which threatened to grow into a full-scale trade war. The whole problem of tariff reductions as proposed by the United States was the subject of a sixty-six nation conference at Geneva in the summer of 1964, under the auspices of the General Agreement on Tariffs and Trade (GATT). This agreement, initiated under UN auspices in 1947, called for periodic conferences among the contracting countries to discuss trade and tariff problems. The "Kennedy round" of discussions, as the Geneva talks were called, while somewhat easing the strain between the United States and the Common Market, stopped far short of the "Atlantic partnership" which had been the late President's goal.

Despite its setbacks in the last few years, the European Economic Community is still a major step forward on the road toward a united Europe. Outside the economic sphere progress toward unity has been far slower. At the time the Schuman Plan was being negotiated, other French proposals called for the military as well as the economic integration of western Europe. In May, 1952, representatives of the ECSC nations met in Paris to sign a treaty establishing a European Defense Community (EDC). Under its provisions each signatory agreed to place its national military contingents under a single supranational command. But this military counterpart of ECSC failed to take into account the deeply rooted fears of the French people of the resurgence of a powerful Germany. These fears were increased when it became clear that Germany insisted on full equality within EDC, and that Great Britain was unwilling to become a member of any such supranational body.

65

After two years of indecisive wrangling the French Assembly in 1954 still refused to ratify the EDC treaty. The problem of German rearmament was finally solved within the framework of the Western Union, or Western European Union (WEU), as it is now called, which has thus gained renewed importance. With Germany and Italy added to the original Brussels Treaty nations, and with its own Council and Assembly, the Western European Union serves a useful purpose in regulating and coordinating the military forces and arms production of its member states. But the Union falls far short of establishing the integrated European army that EDC had envisaged.

Still more disappointing has been the lack of progress made toward European political unity. In May, 1949, under the sponsorship of Europe's most illustrious elder statesman, Winston Churchill, a Council of Europe was set up at Strasbourg for the express purpose of promoting the development of European unity. This Council has a more inclusive membership than either the European Economic Community or the Western European Union. Like those two bodies, it has its own Community of Ministers and Consultative Assembly. But the Council's accomplishments thus far, other than serving as a sounding board, have been negligible. While the EDC treaty was still under discussion, hopes ran high that some supranational political structure might be the next step. In 1953 a constitutional committee actually worked out a draft treaty for a European Political Community that was unanimously adopted by the Strasbourg Assembly. But the failure of EDC upset, for the time being, any hope for political integration. There have been other schemes for political unification since, but none that has received unanimous support. Meanwhile the Council of Europe remains the largest exclusively European body concerned with problems of unity and the most suitable agency for coordinating future efforts in this direction.

Taken as a whole, then, Europe's quest for unity has not been very successful. National differences, traditions, and interests are still powerful obstacles. The blame for the limited progress of European integration has often been laid at the door of Great Britain. Considering herself still primarily a world power rather than a European power, it has been said, Britain hesitates to submit to the restrictions of a United States of Europe. In recent years, however, Britain has shown readiness to draw closer to the nations across the Channel, even to the point of agreeing to the digging of a tunnel underneath that impregnable moat! It has been France, or rather De Gaulle, who has been the major obstacle to such a rapprochement. This is a sad and ironic fact, considering that Frenchmen like Jean Monnet and Robert Schuman have contributed so much to the quest for European unity. The other members of the Common Market, including West Germany, share neither De Gaulle's suspicions of the Anglo-Saxon powers nor his desire for a loose European confederation under French leadership. There is a general awareness, especially among Europe's youth, that the only way in which their continent can reassert itself and exert its full influence in world affairs is by overcoming the divisive issues of petty nationalism and by working for a strong and united Europe within a larger Atlantic community.

3

AMERICA'S LEADERS

A unique photograph of the four men who have occupied
the American presidency since 1945.
The occasion was the funeral of House Speaker
Sam Rayburn in 1961. ASSOCIATED PRESS WIREPHOTO.

THE UNITED STATES
AND ITS
GOOD NEIGHBORS

THE HISTORY OF THE UNITED STATES SINCE
World War II shows that victory in a modern war places before
the victors problems scarcely less complex than those faced by the
vanquished. America was the only one among the major partici-
pants in the war to remain untouched by its devastation. And while
in the past the economic boom caused by the needs of war had
usually subsided with the end of hostilities, this did not happen
in America after World War II. On the contrary, consumer demands, left unfulfilled during the war, and the continued needs
of national defense not only prevented a postwar depression but
led to an unprecedented expansion of America's economy. The
postwar problems that the United States faced, therefore, did not
spring, as in the case of Europe, primarily from economic causes.
America's problems came rather as a result of the sudden demands
for world leadership made against a nation not sufficiently ready

to exercise such leadership. Most Americans expected foreign and national affairs to go back to where they had been when the war started. But this hope was disappointed. The realization that a return to normalcy was impossible gave rise to the air of uncertainty and apprehension that characterized the first postwar years. The way in which Americans finally overcame their difficulties and shouldered their new responsibilities makes the years after 1945 seem less disheartening in retrospect than they appeared at the time.

THE SEARCH FOR A POSTWAR POLICY

The man who was to guide his country through one of its most crucial periods was a well-meaning politician who, upon suddenly becoming President when Franklin D. Roosevelt died on April 12, 1945, "felt like the moon, the stars, and all the planets had fallen on me." With an engaging modesty and a never flagging energy, Harry S. Truman applied himself to his unenviable assignment. During the first months of his new office President Truman assumed the responsibility for decisions, such as the use of the atomic bomb, that would have staggered a more complex personality. But in doing so he still remained for some time to come the mere executor of the policies of his dynamic predecessor. It took a while before the new President began to show signs not merely of leadership but of statesmanship as well.

The most pressing task before the Truman administration was the conversion of the country from warlike to peaceful pursuits. This involved, first of all, the rapid demobilization of nearly nine million men and women. Most of the veterans were either absorbed by industry or took advantage of the farsighted GI Bill of Rights, which aided millions of veterans in starting a business or in gaining a better education. The GI Bill was an important factor in that slow upgrading of American society that was one of the most striking results of the war. Defense industries, paying generously and attracting women as well as men, had also done their share in raising the economic and social level of lower-status groups and in making the majority of Americans decidedly middle class in outlook and aspirations.

While social reconversion was progressing smoothly, economic reconversion proved more difficult. The government tried to hold the line on price controls as long as there was a general shortage of critical items. But postwar price controls aroused the opposition of American business and incidentally helped to perpetuate the ugly practice of black marketeering that had sprung up during the war. At the same time labor, deprived of its income from overtime work, demanded the abolition of wage controls to meet the rising costs of living. When both government and industry stood firm against the lifting of wage controls, labor resorted to large-scale strikes. The effect of strikes was to aggravate shortages and to drive up living costs. These were bewildering times in which the world's richest nation, more prosperous than ever before, was hopelessly caught in the vicious spiral of an inflation for which there seemed no remedy.

There was a similar feeling of bewilderment in America's relations with the outside world. The very fact that foreign affairs did not take a back seat once the war was over but continued to hold the center of the stage was something discomfortingly new. Most Americans had firmly backed their country's war effort and her leading role in the founding of the United Nations. But once the fighting was over, these same people bombarded their congressmen with requests to get their men home as soon as possible. This rapid withdrawal of troops deprived the United States of its major source of influence abroad. It was only the growing threat of communism that gradually made Americans aware of their country's new responsibilities. But if America was to exert her power in world affairs, how and when and where was she to do so? Soviet expansionism was scoring a succession of triumphs, and Soviet obstructionism was crippling the effectiveness of the new United Nations. Yet the United States government seemed to stand by idly, hoping that the Russians might still prove amenable to a reasonable settlement of differences. President Truman, to be sure, had said as early as January, 1946, that he was "tired of babying the Soviets," and he had applauded Winston Churchill's "iron curtain" speech the following March. But the government's policy was still sufficiently aimless that Secretary of Commerce Henry Wallace in September, 1946, could publicly advocate a more cooperative attitude toward the Soviet Union. And while the President's dismissal of Wallace seemed to indicate that the government intended to take a firmer line, specific signs of such firmness were still lacking from America's policy abroad.

In the light of the situation just described, it is not surprising

73

that for the first time in sixteen years the congressional elections of 1946 returned a substantial Republican majority to both houses. Opposition to the Democratic New Deal, of course, had long been present in Republican circles. But with the unsettled conditions of the early postwar years, some of the former supporters and beneficiaries of the Democratic regime also now turned against the administration. The immediate effect of the 1946 elections was to jolt the government into taking a more decisive course. President Truman gave way on the issue of price and wage controls and removed virtually all checks except on rent and some foods. The result was a gradual return of scarce goods and a steady rise in prices. Because the American consumer resisted the temptation of reckless spending, a runaway inflation was avoided. A new policy, initiated by General Motors and adopted by other industries, called for wage contracts that allowed for automatic increases corresponding to rising living costs. This practice went a long way toward pacifying labor unrest. In Congress, on the other hand, labor fared less well. The Taft-Hartley Act of 1947, passed over the President's veto, prohibited the use of union funds for political purposes, introduced a sixty-day notice before a strike or lockout, outlawed the closed shop, and gave the government the right to impose an eighty-day injunction against strikes that imperiled the nation's health and safety. The Labor-Management Act, its official name, at first was violently attacked by the large unions. But their fears that the injunction would be used often and indiscriminately were not realized. In the spring and early summer of 1948 renewed strikes in the coal, steel, and railway industries were successfully resolved by government intervention. At the same time a further round of wage increases was granted to meet the continued rise in the cost of living.

While Congress and the administration failed to see eye to eye on most domestic issues, there was less disagreement in foreign affairs. We have already discussed the various measures, from Truman Doctrine to Marshall Plan, that marked America's initiative in meeting the Soviet threat. Much of the credit for this fresh approach to foreign policy belonged to Secretary of State George C. Marshall and to his deputy, Undersecretary of State Dean Acheson. During 1947 and 1948 the threat of a new war seemed terribly real. Congress already had approved the unification of the armed services under a new Secretary of Defense, and in June, 1948, it passed the first peacetime Selective Service Act in the nation's history. Still, the far-reaching commitments of the Marshall Plan were adopted only over the vehement opposition of the majority of Republicans under the able leadership of Senator Robert A. Taft. They objected to the plan's emphasis on Europe and predicted that it would leave the United States bankrupt. Largely due to the firm support of Senator Arthur H. Vandenberg, the leading Republican member of the Senate Foreign Relations Committee and a man who did not share his party's isolationism, the Foreign Assistance Act (Marshall Plan) was finally passed in March, 1948.

Because of the fumbling record of the Truman administration at home and its too-recent firmness abroad, the outcome of the 1948 presidential election seemed a foregone conclusion. As the South bolted from the Democratic Party, and Henry Wallace further split the Democrats by starting his own "Progressive Party," the Republican candidate, Thomas E. Dewey, seemed certain to win. But the seemingly impossible happened. Contrary to the predictions of various public opinion polls, Harry S. Truman was elected President in his own right, and his party gained a majority in both houses. Many explanations were given for the Republican upset, but in the last analysis Truman was elected because he had the support of the substantial labor bloc, the Negro vote, and at least half the farmers. These were the groups that had profited from the New Deal in the past and that hoped to profit from the Fair Deal that the President announced for the future.

Their hopes were to be only partly fulfilled. The Eighty-first Congress in 1949 passed many of the measures its predecessor had turned down, from public housing and increased minimum wage to farm supports, flood control, and soil conservation. Yet two of the major points of the President's program, the repeal of the Taft-Hartley Act and the enactment of federal civil-rights legislation, failed to win congressional support, largely because of the opposition of the southern Democrats. But the Fair Deal was more than just a domestic program, as President Truman had made clear in the famous Point Four of his inaugural address. In 1949 Congress authorized 5.4 billion dollars for the European Recovery Program, and an additional 3 billion dollars were granted in 1950. Support for these measures came from a coalition of Democrats and Republicans. A similar bipartisan policy insured the passage in July, 1949, of the North Atlantic Treaty, despite the objections of Senator Taft and his supporters that the United States was thus committed to go to war in the defense of western Europe. Thus by early 1949 the United States at long last had regained a measure of stability and was pursuing a policy that had the support of the majority of Americans. At this point a series of events at home and abroad combined to throw the country back into a crisis worse than the one it had just gone through.

THE GROWING FEAR OF COMMUNISM

One of the dominant characteristics of the postwar American climate of opinion was the growing fear of communism, not only abroad but at home. The strength of the American Communist Party, estimated at never more than seventy-five thousand members, was negligible compared to Communist strength in some European countries. But Americans felt that even a small number of Reds in key positions could seriously endanger the nation's security. Beginning in 1946, therefore, a series of congressional investigations were launched, hoping to ferret out possible Communists or their sympathizers from government positions. The careless methods used in these investigations and the harm done to the reputation of innocent people caused deep concern among thoughtful observers. But it became more and more common for an otherwise fair-minded people to condone such methods because of the end they claimed to serve. Several Communists were actually discovered and removed from sensitive positions, but this was done through the government's regular security agencies rather than through congressional investigations. In October, 1949, the eleven leading members of the American Communist Party, after a long and fair trial, were convicted of conspiracy to advocate the violent overthrow of the United States government. The case that caused the greatest stir, however, was that of Alger Hiss, formerly of the State Department, who was found guilty of having falsely denied under oath his former Communist affiliations and activities. There still remained people who refused to believe that Hiss was guilty. But to the majority of Americans, this well-born, well-educated, and well-connected young man symbolized the very treason they suspected in high places.

In this suspicion they were confirmed by Wisconsin's Republican Senator Joseph McCarthy. This ambitious politician had long sought an opportunity to gain nationwide publicity. Such an opportunity arose with the growing panic about communism in the government. The Senator's main target was the United States State Department and in particular Dean Acheson, Secretary of State since 1949. In a speech at Wheeling, West Virginia, in 1950, McCarthy asserted that he had a list of 205 Communist Party members or sympathizers still employed by the State Department. These claims were subsequently proved false. But this did not concern the Senator and the growing number of his supporters. In 1951 McCarthy directed his attacks against General Marshall, whom he accused of participating in a conspiracy "to the end that we shall be contained, frustrated and finally fall victim to Soviet intrigue from within and Russian military might from without." Instead of dissociating themselves from such indiscriminate mud-slinging, more and more respectable Republicans lined up with their colleague who so correctly seemed to gauge the temper of the nation. Congress had just passed the sweeping Internal Security Act of 1950, which required Communists and Communist-front organizations to register with the Justice Department. President Truman's unsuccessful attempt to veto this act was construed as further evidence of his softness toward communism.

THE WAR IN KOREA

The reality of the Communist threat, meanwhile, was brought home anew by events in Korea. We have already discussed the outbreak of the Korean war on June 24, 1950, and the intervention of the United States under the auspices of the United Nations. The firm stand taken by President Truman briefly united the country as it had not been united since the end of World War II. Even Senator Taft, while criticizing the administration's earlier Korean policy, supported the President. But as the Korean war bogged down into a bloody stalemate, the initial unity soon disappeared. It was over the discussion of how to break this stalemate that the United States was thrown into its most serious domestic crisis since World War II.

Disagreement over American Far Eastern policy had been of long standing. The government was aware of Asian sensibilities and wanted to avoid anything remotely smacking of colonialism. It had, therefore, repeatedly opposed the use of force on the Asiatic mainland and proposed instead to win native support and contain communism through economic and technical assistance. Yet such a

77

policy, its critics charged, was not only slow and expensive, but, as China and Korea had shown, ineffective. Some opponents of the administration went still further and saw America's Asian policy as merely another manifestation of the pro-Communist leanings of which they accused the administration. Instead of diverting so much American money and manpower to Europe, these critics advocated all-out economic and military aid to those nations of Asia, in particular Nationalist China, that were engaged in fighting communism. This "Asia First" program appealed to many Americans as the best way of halting the creeping advance of communism. The program's popularity was further assured by the support it received from General Douglas MacArthur, a man long actively involved in Far Eastern affairs.

MacArthur at the start of the Korean war had advocated the use of Chinese Nationalist troops against North Korea. At that time he had been opposed by Dean Acheson for political reasons and by the Joint Chiefs of Staff on military grounds. Now that the war had frozen into a stalemate, MacArthur repeated his earlier proposal. He also emphasized the need for a blockade of the Chinese coast and the bombing of Communist bases beyond the Yalu River to insure an early victory. President Truman, together with his political and military advisers, considered MacArthur's scheme dangerous, since it might lead to a major war in which America would not have the support of her allies. Despite repeated warnings to desist, MacArthur nevertheless continued in his open criticism of the government's policy. Seeing no alternative, President Truman on April 11, 1951, relieved MacArthur of all his commands.

The news of MacArthur's dismissal caused a storm of indignation. The uneasy suspicion that America's fate was in the hands of incompetents, if not traitors, suddenly seemed to be borne out. The issue appeared joined in the contest between a man whom his opponents still considered a small-time politician from Missouri and the nation's most glamorous military hero. The real issue of the military's subordination to civilian control was somehow overlooked. While MacArthur staged a triumphant return, demands were heard for the impeachment of the President and his Secretary of State. But after a few weeks the furor gradually died down. The President's popularity, to be sure, never recovered from the blow it had suffered. But President Truman's loss did not become MacArthur's gain. The general did not become the rallying point of the opposition, as his supporters had hoped, but kept his promise to "just fade away." He died, a much honored though still controversial figure, in 1964.

The Korean war, besides making enemies for the Democratic administration, also made itself felt in other ways. Economically, it brought to the United States the greatest wave of prosperity ever. Employment set new records, and business profits soared. But with prosperity came further inflation, and those sections of the population with fixed incomes failed to share in the nation's new wealth. As is often the case in times of plenty, corruption became a common practice. These were the days of the "five percenters," when deep freezes and mink coats seemed to have become the accepted bribes in paying government employees for favors granted. A special committee under Senator Estes Kefauver of Tennessee uncovered mountains of evidence on the political influence of crime syndicates in various large communities, especially New York City. In addition, juvenile delinquency for the first time became a national problem.

A country thus agitated by scandals at home and a costly and inconclusive war abroad was in no mood for dealing judiciously with the barrage of falsehoods and half-truths issuing from those who, like Senator McCarthy, hoped to make political capital out of the nation's bewilderment. If there was one thing on which most Americans seemed to agree, it was the desire for a change in the government. The 1950 elections brought a first decline of Democratic strength in Congress. But the major change did not come until 1952. The elections of that year were unique in many respects. Rarely had there been a more important contest. Yet the candidates selected by each party were complete novices in the realm of high party and national politics. The Democratic nominee, Illinois governor Adlai E. Stevenson, carrying the burden of an unpopular administration, conducted a distinguished campaign, marked by speeches of unusual intelligence. But it was the Republican candidate, Dwight D. Eisenhower, a successful general but a political amateur, who won the election. The Eisenhower platform, with its slogan that it was "time for a change" and with its promise "to clean up the mess in Washington," seemed to express the feelings of the majority of Americans. The Republican victory in the presidential contest was a landslide and a personal triumph for General Eisenhower, who carried thirty-nine states. On the congressional side the success of the Republicans was less spectacular, as they won only slim majorities in both houses. Yet there was a general feeling that after twenty years of Democratic rule a new era had dawned in American politics. The question was whether its tone would be set by the man who had won the election or by the party that had nominated him.

THE EISENHOWER ERA

President Eisenhower's most powerful contender for the Republican nomination had been "Mr. Republican" himself, Senator Robert A. Taft. And while the two had outwardly adjusted their differences for the sake of party unity, once the elections were over, Taft's conservative influence made itself strongly felt, even beyond his untimely death in 1953. The Taft influence was shown in the composition of the new cabinet, in which businessmen and outspoken believers in free enterprise were given key positions. As a result, business rallied to support the government as it had not done in two decades. One of the Republican campaign promises had been to balance the budget and to reduce taxes. Efforts were made to cut government spending. But the continued drain of military spending at home and military as well as economic aid abroad made any radical tax relief impossible. In an effort to return to a free market in agricultural products, the government replaced the rigid price supports of the past with more flexible ones. The administration thus incurred the opposition of farm groups. The trend toward greater freedom from federal control also came out in other measures. Some of these, such as the transfer to state jurisdiction of tidelands oil and the emphasis on private, rather than public, development of natural resources, were branded as "giveaways" by the Democratic opposition. In the elections of 1954 Democratic charges that the government was run for the benefit of the large corporations rather than the little man helped to bring a Democratic majority to both houses of Congress. There also was some fear at the time that America's economy had overexpanded and was headed for a depression. But such fears proved groundless. One of the major developments in American domestic affairs came in May, 1954, when the Supreme Court handed down a ruling outlawing segregation in the nation's public schools. While in some states school integration, beginning in 1955, proceeded smoothly, most of the southern states announced that they would use every peaceful means at their disposal to oppose integration.

While the Eisenhower administration thus pursued a new course in domestic affairs, its foreign policy generally continued along the lines of its predecessor. The new Secretary of State, John Foster Dulles, had served as Republican adviser on foreign affairs during the Truman era. As such he had supported America's far-flung military and economic involvements. Yet the growing cost of these commitments increasingly came under attack from the followers of Senator Taft. On the other hand, the administration's efforts to trim its military budget by reducing the Army's ground forces and by using atomic weapons instead of men for "massive retaliation" were criticized by experts as weakening America's ability to halt the advance of communism in a limited war, as had been done in Korea. The termination of fighting in Korea shortly after President Eisenhower took office was claimed as a victory for his administration's firmness in dealing with the Chinese Communists. The change in Russian policy, following the death of Stalin in March, 1953, may also have had something to do with ending the Korean impasse.

With a change in national leadership it might have been expected that the American people would lose their fear of Communist infiltration at home. But with a Republican majority in Congress until 1954 Senator McCarthy at long last had his day. As chairman of the important Senate Committee on Government Operations and of its Permanent Subcommittee on Investigations, the Senator now embarked on a series of investigations that became increasingly embarrassing to the Eisenhower administration. He first turned his spotlight on the State Department's overseas information service and in particular on its American libraries abroad. The result was a general purging of all works by "Communists, fellow-travelers, etc.," causing the removal, and in some instances the burning, of books by authors who were free from any Communist taint. Such actions brought charges at home and abroad that America was trying to combat totalitarianism by totalitarian methods. At the beginning of 1954 McCarthy shifted his attentions to the Army, making the usual accusations of Communist infiltration. The nationally televised Army-McCarthy hearings showed the Wisconsin Senator at his most arrogant. The outcome of the hearings, while not entirely absolving the Army, still was sufficiently damaging to McCarthy for the Senate to pass a carefully worded move of censure against him. Soon afterward, the chairmanship of McCarthy's committees changed hands as a consequence of the 1954 elections, and the Senator suddenly found himself relegated to obscurity. The nightmare of "McCarthyism" was over, although its effects were felt for years to come.

The defeat of McCarthy completed the process by which President Eisenhower emancipated himself from the Republican old guard, many of whom had sided with the Wisconsin Senator. The President's popularity, which had helped win the election in 1952, continued to be one of the Republicans' major assets. There was never any doubt that the party wanted him to run again. The Democratic nominee in 1956 was again Adlai Stevenson, who carried on a vigorous campaign. The Republicans were content to stand on a record of "peace, prosperity, and progress." The outcome of the 1956 elections was a still greater landslide victory for Eisenhower than he had won four years earlier. But while the President carried forty-one states, the Democrats retained control of both houses of Congress. President Eisenhower's victory, therefore, was a personal triumph. He himself, however, modestly interpreted it as a sign "that modern Republicanism has now proved itself, and America has approved of modern Republicanism."

President Eisenhower's "modern Republicanism" has been described as "liberalism in terms of people's needs, conservatism in terms of their money." The President took a positive stand on moderate expansion of the government's social role, he favored federal aid to education, and he supported integration and civil rights. But he remained firm in his opposition to excessive spending and to subsidies that might lead to further inflation. Faced by a Democratic majority in Congress throughout his second term, Eisenhower's hands were tied on some partisan issues. But just as often as not, Democrats and Republicans were divided within their own ranks—conservatives against liberals—and collaboration between the liberal elements in both parties resulted in some constructive legislation. The government's foreign policy, at least until shortly before the end of the Eisenhower era, had the support of the majority of Americans.

President Eisenhower himself, in contrast to Roosevelt and Truman, remained remarkably free from personal attacks. His distinguished military career, his evident sincerity, and his friendly manner earned him the affection of most Americans. Only toward the end did his popularity begin to decline, as some critics found him wanting in leadership at a time of national crisis. Eisenhower's delicate health was partly responsible for this, since it narrowly circumscribed his activities. Aggressive leadership at home, moreover, was foreign to the President's nature and contrary to his conception of the presidential office. And finally, the fact that he was the first President to have his tenure limited to two terms under the Twenty-second Amendment could not help weakening his power and effectiveness. Many of Eisenhower's responsibilities, especially during his several illnesses, were taken over by Vice-President Richard Nixon, who thus increased his own stature as well as that of his office.

The record of any administration depends to a large extent upon the success of its economic policy. The United States continued to prosper under Eisenhower, as it had under Truman, until by early 1960 the nation's gross national product—the dollar value of goods and services—reached the magic mark of 500 billion dollars, or half a trillion. Despite continued production records, however, the nation's economy showed some weak spots. There had been a marked recession in 1958, and the rate of growth since then had been slow. The number of jobless continued to be about 5 per cent of the total labor force, a disquieting figure for a period of prosperity. The farm picture did not look much better. With continued surpluses driving down prices, farm income continued to drop, while living costs and interest rates were going up. As fewer farmers were producing more crops on less land, due to improvements in agricultural techniques, the only real solution seemed to be for some farmers to seek a livelihood in something other than agriculture.

While America's economy thus had its weaknesses, it nevertheless continued to grow. By mid-1960 more persons were employed than at any time in American history. As had happened in earlier periods of prosperity, public morality became lax, and the Eisenhower administration was not spared its share of scandals. A special House subcommittee charged with looking into the operations of the government's regulatory agencies uncovered abundant evidence of unethical practices and forced the resignation of several commissioners who had accepted favors from the business interests they were supposed to regulate. The inquiry that caused the greatest stir dealt with "payola," that is, the payment of money or goods to broadcasters for "plugging" a certain product. The public was particularly shocked when it learned that many of its favorite quiz programs on radio and television had been "fixed." Here was an indication that corruption was not confined to the government but extended to other institutions of a semi-public nature such as the communications industry.

The labor unions fall into a similar category. With a total

membership of more than eighteen million, the unions not only wield great political and economic power, but their huge funds make them a fruitful field for corruption. In 1957 a Senate committee uncovered evidence of widespread fraud among labor officials. In one case at least, the International Brotherhood of Teamsters, the misuse of funds was so flagrant that this largest of all unions was expelled from the AFL-CIO. To impose stricter control upon organized labor and to curb some of its more arbitrary actions, Congress in 1959 passed a new labor law. Under its provisions unions must file regular financial reports, must disclose their administrative procedures, and must bar former convicts from holding office. Union members are protected against leadership abuses by a "bill of rights." The "secondary boycott"—that is, a union's effort to put pressure on one employer by striking against another with whom he has dealings—was made more difficult and picketing was outlawed under certain circumstances. But while the new law did away with some of the worst practices of corrupt unionism, it did little to curtail the power of the stronger unions.

The most important domestic concern of the Eisenhower administration was over the related issues of desegregation and civil rights. The deep South had resisted from the start the Supreme Court's decision on school integration handed down in 1954. The most serious fight against integration took place in Little Rock, Arkansas, where federal troops had to be used in order to protect the handful of Negro students who insisted on their right to attend a hitherto all-white school. By 1960 little more than one-fourth of the South's 2,850 biracial school districts had been desegregated on even a token basis. Meanwhile a campaign of passive resistance among Negroes was carrying the fight for integration beyond the field of education. A strike against segregated buses in Montgomery, Alabama, was won in 1958; and peaceful "sit-in" demonstrations in 1960 resulted in the opening of lunch counters to Negroes in some parts of the South. Efforts to secure Negro rights by means of civil-rights legislation were at least partly successful. The Civil Rights Act of 1957 reaffirmed the right of the Negro to vote, and the Civil Rights Act of 1960 provided the necessary safeguards to make sure that this right was enforced. Attempts to widen the scope of legislation to include school integration and equal job opportunities, however, ran into staunch opposition from southern senators who fought even the slight concessions made in the first civil-rights measures passed since Reconstruction days.

We shall discuss America's foreign policy during the 1950's at greater length below (see Chapter 6). Its underlying concern and the subject of endless debates at home was the continued rivalry between the United States and Russia, especially in such important fields as military strength, scientific development, and economic growth. With more than half of its budget devoted to military spending, the United States concentrated its efforts upon closing the "missile gap" which still gave the Soviet Union a lead in long-range intercontinental ballistic missiles. The military rivalry between the United States and Russia was in the final analysis a contest between the scientists of both countries. The most spectacular side of this contest was the race for the exploration of outer space. Here, too, the Russians held a commanding lead, not only by being the first to launch an earth satellite, but by putting far heavier satellites into orbit than the United States and by outdoing the Americans in shots to the moon. In the light of Russia's scientific achievements, Premier Khrushchev's prediction that his country would some day surpass the United States economically could not be dismissed as an empty boast. In 1960 American production was still unsurpassed, with a gross national product twice that of the U.S.S.R. But to keep this lead it was estimated that the United States economy would have to grow at the rate of at least 5 per cent each year. And there were those who doubted that this rate of growth could be maintained.

Among the main charges leveled by the Democrats against the Eisenhower administration in the election campaigns of 1958 and 1960 was lack of leadership in foreign and domestic affairs. The congressional elections of 1958 brought a sweeping victory for the opposition, with Democratic majorities approaching two-thirds in both houses. Aware of how much was at stake in the presidential contest of 1960, both parties nominated unusually able contenders. Both the Republican candidate, Richard M. Nixon, and the Democratic nominee, John F. Kennedy, were cool-headed, tough-minded, and articulate young men. The platforms on which they ran were remarkable more for their similarities than for their differences. The campaign, therefore, was less a contest of issues than of personalities. The outcome of the presidential race was extremely close. John F. Kennedy won a clear victory of electoral votes, but the popular vote was narrowly divided. The new president was the first Catholic and the youngest candidate ever to be elected to the White House. With Congress remaining under

Democratic control, Kennedy could look forward to carrying out his bold and imaginative program of the "New Frontier."

THE NEW FRONTIER— FROM KENNEDY TO JOHNSON

The New Frontier was both a credo and a program. It was a profession of faith in America's future and an appeal to the American people to help realize that future. "Ask not what your country can do for you, ask what you can do for your country"—so ran the most frequently quoted passage from President Kennedy's inaugural address. People seemed ready to respond to this call "to get the country going again," even though it was not quite clear what, specifically, was expected of them. The program of the new administration called for far-reaching social and economic measures at home and for continued American leadership of the free world. Since the New Frontier envisaged more rather than less government control and more rather than less government spending, it could expect opposition from the conservative forces in Congress.

The New Frontier got off to a good start. By the end of 1961 Congress had passed a series of social service measures, including a multi-billion-dollar housing bill, a depressed areas bill, and a minimum wage law. But these measures by and large continued policies initiated by earlier administrations. When it came to striking out into new directions, on the other hand, the Kennedy administration soon ran into difficulties. High on the President's program were federal aid to education, medical care for the aged, a Department of Urban Affairs, more rigid controls over surplus farm products, tax reduction, and civil rights. On none of these issues did Kennedy have his way. Compromises were reached on a few points, but these fell far short of what the President had hoped for. The Democrats maintained their lead in the 1962 elections. But congressional voting on most issues was along ideological, rather than party, lines, with liberals of both parties supporting the administration, and conservatives opposing it. Within Kennedy's own party, the main opposition to the President's program came from the powerful bloc of southern Democrats. The main reason for their obstruction was the administration's strong stand on civil rights.

The President had proceeded warily on this touchy subject,

86

preferring at first to aid the Negro through executive action rather than federal legislation. An exception was the constitutional amendment of 1962, barring the poll tax in federal elections. It was not until 1963 that a comprehensive civil rights bill was sent to Congress, where it ran into solid southern opposition. The Negro community, meanwhile, pressed its claims for equality through nonviolent action—public demonstrations, sit-ins, and freedom marches. The most impressive such demonstration came in August, 1963, when some two hundred thousand people staged an orderly "March on Washington" to demand "Freedom Now!" In the deep South, however, the situation became increasingly explosive, as police action turned peaceful demonstrations into violent riots, and white opponents of integration used every means, including arson and murder, to delay the inevitable. From the South Negro protests spread to the North, demanding better job opportunities and an end to de facto segregation of schools and housing.

President Kennedy's stand on civil rights, by causing southern opposition, was partly responsible for the failure of the rest of his domestic program. Another reason for this failure was the President's absorption in foreign affairs. Beginning shortly after his inauguration, Kennedy was faced with a series of crises—in Southeast Asia, Cuba, and Berlin—which never let up during his brief period in office. We shall discuss the details of these crises elsewhere. Some of them, notably the failure of the Cuban invasion in April, 1961, brought considerable criticism at home. But on most foreign policy questions the President enjoyed bipartisan support. His foreign program fared far better in Congress than his domestic one. Requests for foreign aid were granted without drastic cuts, at least until 1963. Defense appropriations were greater at times than what the administration had asked for. The same applied to the space program which aimed at landing a man on the moon by 1970. In 1962 Congress passed the Trade Expansion Act, which gave the President unprecedented powers for cutting tariffs; and in 1963 it ratified the treaty banning nuclear tests. Another measure, the founding of the Peace Corps, an organization which in some ways reflected the idealism generated by the New Frontier, likewise received bipartisan congressional support.

In his foreign policy President Kennedy certainly could not complain about insufficient legislative support. There were critics, of course, who accused the administration of being "too soft" and who proposed to "get tough" with the Communists. But the majority of Americans seemed ready to go along with the President's rule: "never negotiate out of fear, but . . . never fear to negotiate." Kennedy's popularity, throughout his brief presidency, remained high; only toward the end were there signs of some decline. The business community opposed him, especially after a showdown with the steel industry in 1962 over a projected price increase for steel, which Kennedy successfully prevented. But business opposition hardly hurt the President's popularity. Most Americans obviously liked the bright and eager young man in the White House who brought a new style and a new freshness into the national government. There certainly was little doubt that Kennedy would be re-elected in 1964.

President Kennedy was assassinated in Dallas, Texas, on November 22, 1963. The man charged with the murder, Lee Harvey Oswald, was himself assassinated before he could be tried. The nation and the world experienced a wave of shock and grief such as had rarely, if ever, been felt before. A major crisis was avoided chiefly because of the firm and confident manner in which President Kennedy's successor stepped in to take command. Lyndon B. Johnson had fought hard to get the presidency for himself in 1960. Yet after he was defeated, he had served loyally and ably as Vice-President under Kennedy. A skillful politician, known for his belief in reasonableness and persuasion, Johnson had many friends in Congress, where he had worked with distinction for many years, last as Senate majority leader. The nation and the world were fortunate that so able a man stood ready to shoulder so difficult a task.

There were few changes in policy and personnel as President Johnson pledged continuation of his predecessor's program. Yet where Kennedy had labored long and in vain to make headway against congressional opposition, Johnson was able to achieve a number of quick successes. Some of these achievements—passage of the foreign aid bill, the tax cut bill, and the civil-rights bill—were legacies from the Kennedy days, and credit for them belongs to both men. But President Johnson struck out on his own when he declared his "war on poverty" and had his declaration implemented by congressional action in a number of important areas. In April, 1964, the President scored a major personal triumph by helping to settle a five-year-old railroad dispute through collective bargaining. Relations between business and the government under Johnson took a decided turn for the better, as the President stressed his desire for economy in government and his support of any measure that assured continuation of the nation's economic boom. Abroad the Johnson administration was faced by the same troubles that had beset Kennedy and, for that matter, Eisenhower. There were more flare-ups with Cuba, renewed trouble in Cyprus and the Congo, and fresh anti-American outbreaks in Panama. Foreign affairs was the area with which the new President had been least familiar in the past. But here, too, Johnson soon showed a firm grasp of complex issues, thus winning the trust of America's friends and the respect of her foes.

By the summer of 1964 President Johnson had gained sufficent stature as a political leader to make him a difficult person to beat in the fall elections. Still, the Republicans had a number of capable candidates, any one of whom might have proved a serious contender for the presidency if backed by the rank and file of his party. But the GOP had long been split. We have seen how during the Eisenhower era old-guard republicanism had been overshadowed by a more modern, liberal brand of republicanism. The conservative wing of the party had survived, however, and had actually gained in strength. This was shown at the Republican convention in 1964, when the leader of the conservatives, Senator Barry Goldwater of Arizona, was chosen as his party's candidate. This choice was opposed by the liberal wing of the party. But there was hope that its possible defection would be balanced by an equal defection from Democratic ranks over the civil-rights question.

By the fall of 1964, civil rights had become the key issue in American domestic politics. The Civil Rights Act of 1964 was the most sweeping legislation of its kind to date. It outlawed racial discrimination in places of public accomodation; it authorized the federal government to intervene on behalf of victims of discrimination; it forbade racial discrimination by employers and unions; and it assured equal voting rights to whites and Negroes. Passage of the Civil Rights Act was preceded by a long filibuster of southern senators. The provision against discrimination in public accommodations was the most fought-over portion of the new law. While there was compliance with the rights bill in many parts of the South, there was defiance in others. The governor of Alabama called the measure "a fraud, a sham and a hoax," and the governor of Mississippi advised resistance against the law until its constitutionality had been tested in the courts. In the North, meanwhile,

89

Negro riots in Harlem, Brooklyn, Rochester, and other urban centers underscored the urgent need for radical improvement of the underprivileged status of most colored citizens. The new Civil Rights Act was of little importance there, since its provisions had long been legally in force in the northern states. What was needed was action against de facto inequalities in employment, housing, and education.

The presidential campaign of 1964 was a heated one. The two candidates clashed on every major issue, with Senator Goldwater accusing the Johnson administration of moral laxity and socialism at home and defeatism abroad, and President Johnson charging his opponent with extremism and general irresponsibility. As many moderate Republicans, the press, and some business interests turned against Goldwater, the outcome of the election was never much in doubt. President Johnson won a landslide victory, and the Democrats maintained their majority in both houses of Congress.

THE UNITED STATES AND CANADA

The most important country in the Americas, next to the United States, is Canada. Larger in size than its southern neighbor, but with a population of only 19 million, this sovereign member of the (British) Commonwealth has made such amazing progress since World War II that she ranks today as one of the world's major industrial and commercial powers. The recent development of her vast resources of iron ore, oil, and especially uranium have opened unlimited vistas of future growth, from which not only Canada herself but also the United States can expect to profit. The United States has already invested close to 20 billion dollars in Canadian resources and industries. This figure represents more than one-third of total American investments abroad and about three-quarters of the foreign capital invested in Canada. Commercial relations between the United States and Canada exceed in volume those between any other two nations. A major step in United States–Canadian collaboration came with the opening in 1959 of the St. Lawrence Seaway and Power Project, which is an important boon to transportation and industry in both countries. Aside from her economic importance, Canada is of the greatest strategic value to the United States as an ally in the cold war. As far back as 1940 the two nations initiated a united program of military planning through a Permanent Joint Defense Committee. In 1950 Canada supported the United Nations in the Korean war with naval, air, and ground forces. As a member of NATO, Canada is also involved in the defense of Europe. She has collaborated with the United States in the construction of three lines of radar installations to provide protection against a polar attack upon the North American continent: the Distant Early Warning (DEW) line, the Mid-Canada line, and the Pinetree line. And she has joined the United States in the creation of the North American Air Defense Command (NORAD).

Despite the close economic, military, and cultural ties between the two neighbors, Canada's feelings toward the United States in recent years have not always been too cordial. In the parliamentary elections of 1957 the middle-of-the-road Liberal Party was ousted from power after an unbroken reign of twenty-two years. The victory of the Progressive Conservatives, led by John Diefenbaker, was due to their emphasis on Canadian nationalism, chiefly at the expense of the United States. Refusal of the Diefenbaker government to incorporate nuclear warheads into Canada's defenses under joint United States–Canadian control again led to its fall in 1963. But the return of the Liberals under Lester B. Pearson was by a narrow margin only. Canadians have been worried for some time over the growing influence of the United States in their country's affairs, and have feared that Canada might lose her identity and become a dependency of the United States. The fact that Canada suffers a sizeable yearly deficit in its trade with the United States, and the charge that the United States program for the disposal of surplus farm products cuts into Canada's wheat trade makes for added strain. It is not that Canadians have become violently anti-American so much as that they have become more pro-Canadian.

This new spirit of self-confidence and independence showed itself not only in Canada's dealings with the United States but also in her relations with Great Britain. Canada is still a loyal member of the Commonwealth. But this has not kept her from pursuing an independent course, as she did during the Suez crisis in 1956, when UN intervention in Egypt was due largely to Canadian initiative. The controversy over the adoption of a new flag that would dispense with the traditional Union Jack, and the cool reception given Queen Elizabeth during her State visit in 1964 in parts of Canada were evidence of strong anti-British resentment,

91

especially among French-Canadians. Still, Great Britain continues to be Canada's second most important customer, and Canada profits greatly from the preferential treatment she receives on the British market as a member of the Commonwealth. Continued close ties with the former mother country and the Commonwealth, furthermore, may be one way of saving Canada from becoming engulfed by her powerful neighbor to the south.

LATIN AMERICA IN TRANSITION

The history of Latin America since World War II has been a succession of political revolutions, economic crises, and social upheaval. The root of this unrest is poverty. Like the peoples of Asia and Africa, the masses of Latin America need to gain at least a minimum of economic security before they can hope to achieve political stability. To make use of their ample resources and thus escape their poverty, the twenty nations of Central and South America not only need outside aid, but they also have to learn to cooperate with each other more closely than they have in the past. To bring about such harmony within the Western Hemisphere has been one of the aims of United States foreign policy. It has been made difficult in recent years because of a strong upsurge of Latin American nationalism, encouraged at times by Communist agitation.

Politically Latin America has long been known for its instability, with dictators following one another in rapid succession. After World War II the trend seemed to be in a more peaceful and orderly direction. Beginning with Argentina's Juan Perón in 1955, one after another of the traditional strong men were overthrown—in Colombia, Peru, Venezuela, and Cuba—until by 1960 only the Dominican Republic, Paraguay, Nicaragua, and Haiti were still ruled by traditional dictators. Cuba was in a category by itself. Here the old-style dictatorship of Fulgencio Batista gave way in 1959 to the revolutionary dictatorship of Fidel Castro, which since then has become Communist in all but name.

Yet even where representative institutions existed in Latin America, democracy was often mixed with authoritarianism. Lack of political experience, educational backwardness, and staggering economic problems made any parliamentary government, as we know it, impossible. In most countries the government in the

1950's and early 1960's was run by the growing middle class, industrial and commercial interests backed by the military and the Catholic Church. Under the leadership of men like Arturo Frondizi of Argentina, Juscelino Kubitschek of Brazil, Rómuló Betancourt of Venezuela, and Alberto Lleras Camargo of Colombia, these middle-of-the-road moderates tried to solve their nations' problems by gradual democratic means. But in many countries their rule was being challenged by the more radical masses, often left-wing and always ultranationalist. They look to the example of Cuba and Fidel Castro as a way out of their economic difficulties. Nationalism is nothing new in Latin America, and for some time past its favorite target has been the United States. But it is only in recent years that Latin American nationalism has taken the violent form of anti-United States riots and demonstrations against visiting American dignitaries. In some instances ultranationalism has led to the confiscation of foreign holdings, beginning as far back as 1938 with the seizure of American oil properties in Mexico and culminating in the more recent wave of expropriations in Cuba. Latin American nationalism has proved a useful weapon in the hands of Communist agitators. The importance of communism in Latin America is far out of proportion to the small number of its registered followers. Even though the Communist Party has been outlawed in more than half of the republics, its influence is felt throughout Central and South America. By infiltrating student and labor organizations, Latin America's Communists, under orders from Moscow, have been responsible for most of the anti-American demonstrations in recent years. There are Communists in the parliaments of at least six countries, and in Cuba Communists and their sympathizers are determining national policy.

Partly because of the real or alleged threat of communism, partly because democratic regimes proved incapable of coping with the social and political ferment of the masses, there has been a reversion toward dictatorship in several Latin American countries in recent years. In 1963 military juntas took control in Guatemala, Ecuador, Honduras, and the Dominican Republic. The overthrow of the firmly entrenched dictatorship of Rafael Trujillo in the Dominican Republic in 1961 had been hailed as a major victory of the trend toward democracy in Latin America. The overthrow of the new regime two years later came as a severe shock to the free world. In several other countries the situation is far from stable. In Venezuela the moderate government of Raul Leoni is

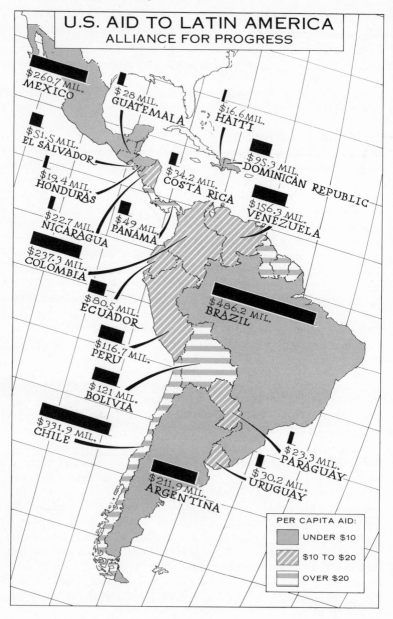

U.S. AID TO LATIN AMERICA
ALLIANCE FOR PROGRESS

$260.7 MIL.
MEXICO

$28 MIL.
GUATEMALA

$16.6 MIL.
HAITI

$51.5 MIL.
EL SALVADOR

$34.2 MIL.
COSTA RICA

$95.3 MIL.
DOMINICAN REPUBLIC

$19.4 MIL.
HONDURAS

$156.3 MIL.
VENEZUELA

$22.7 MIL.
NICARAGUA

$49 MIL.
PANAMA

$237.3 MIL.
COLOMBIA

$80.5 MIL.
ECUADOR

$486.2 MIL.
BRAZIL

$116.7 MIL.
PERU

$121 MIL.
BOLIVIA

$331.9 MIL.
CHILE

$23.3 MIL.
PARAGUAY

$30.2 MIL.
URUGUAY

$211.9 MIL.
ARGENTINA

PER CAPITA AID:

UNDER $10

$10 TO $20

OVER $20

© 1964 by The New York Times Company. Reprinted by permission.

UNDERDEVELOPED ECONOMIES

MEXICO

GUATEMALA
COFFEE 60%
EL SALVADOR
COFFEE 61.1%
COSTA RICA
PANAMA
COLOMBIA
COFFEE 71%

BR. HONDURAS
HONDURAS
NICARAGUA
BANANAS 54.5%

CUBA
HAITI
DOMINICAN REPUBLIC
PUERTO RICO

VENEZUELA
OIL 92%

BRITISH GUIANA
SURINAM
FRENCH GUIANA

ECUADOR

PERU

B R A Z I L

BOLIVIA
TIN 68.5%

PARAGUAY

CHILE
COPPER 65.7%

ARGENTINA

URUGUAY
WOOL 62.9%

PER CAPITA NATIONAL INCOME

UNDER $200 $200 TO $400

OVER $400

MAIN EXPORTS ARE SHOWN FOR
NATIONS RECEIVING MORE THAN HALF
OF EXPORT EARNINGS FROM ONE
PRODUCT. PERCENTS SHOW
PROPORTION OF TOTAL EXPORTS.

faced by strong agitation from the left, aided by Cuba. Peru suffers from extremist peasant revolts; Bolivia is in a state of constant political unrest; and British Guiana, while awaiting independence from the mother country, is ruled by a Marxist premier and is divided by racial strife. The situation in Brazil, largest and potentially most powerful of the South American states, looked up in early 1964 when a gradual drift to the left was halted by the overthrow of President João Goulart and the establishment of a moderate democratic regime. But Brazil's economic and financial situation remains precarious at best.

The underlying cause of Latin American unrest, as was pointed out above, is poverty. It has become more dismal since World War II because of the alarming increase in population. Improvements in health and sanitation have been chiefly responsible for this unprecedented acceleration, which shows no sign of abating. The population of Latin America in 1965 is estimated at more than two hundred million, and if the present rate of growth continues, that number in another generation will be more than double. The result of this population explosion has been a steady lowering of per capita income. In 1965 the average annual income in half the Latin American republics was less than two hundred dollars, and in Bolivia and Haiti it was below one hundred dollars. Vast differences in the economic status of a privileged few and the dismal poverty of the masses is a constant source of social and political unrest. Latin America has tremendous economic potentialities. Yet the development of these potentialities is still only in its early stages. Natural resources, except for oil, have hardly begun to be developed. Agriculture, to become more productive, requires the aid of large public projects for irrigation, storage, and improved transportation. Another need is for economic planning, providing for greater diversification and eliminating duplication among different nations. Eleven of the Latin American countries at present receive more than half their export earnings from only one commodity. Any fluctuation in the world market price of that commodity, therefore, has the most serious repercussions. With many nations specializing in the same products, furthermore, competition is keen and trade within Latin America is negligible. Finally, economic reform, to be effective, calls for the education of the masses, millions of whom are still illiterate.

The governments of Latin America have made some efforts to solve their economic problems by self-help and collaboration. The small republics of Central America have taken steps toward a common market, along the lines of the European Economic Community. But lack of transportation facilities, currency differences, and overlapping of national products make this a difficult task. Some progress has been made in regulating competition among the fifteen coffee-producing nations. In 1958 President Kubitschek of Brazil put forth a major development program, "Operation Pan-America." But such an ambitious scheme required vast amounts of capital, and such funds Latin America did not have. Most of the countries suffer from chronic inflation and run yearly deficits, even without any major public works programs. The capital for economic development, therefore, has to come from the outside. And here Latin America is looking first and foremost to the United States.

THE UNITED STATES AND LATIN AMERICA

Ever since the early nineteenth century and the proclamation of the Monroe Doctrine, relations with her neighbors in Central and South America have been of major concern to the United States. In the years before World War II it was customary to refer to America's relations with Latin America as a "good neighbor policy" and to the spirit animating that policy as "Pan-Americanism." Since World War II, however, the growing involvement of the United States in world affairs has reduced the relative significance of the Western Hemisphere countries in the general scheme of United States foreign policy. As a result, the countries to the south have come to feel neglected by their powerful northern neighbor. At the same time the threat of Communist aggression from within and without has made continued inter-American solidarity more important than ever.

To present a united front against this threat, the nations of the Western Hemisphere—all except Canada, Nicaragua, and Ecuador—signed the Inter-American Treaty of Reciprocal Assistance (Rio Treaty) at the Rio de Janeiro Conference in 1947. Its Articles 3 and 6 provide that "an attack by any state against an American state shall be considered as an attack against all," and that the signatories shall consult on joint action "if the inviolability or the integrity of the territory or the sovereignty or political independence of any American state should be affected by an

97

aggression which is not an armed attack." The latter provision was broad enough to cover a possible Communist attack from within. It was elaborated by the Caracas Declaration of 1954, which specifically stated that the spread of communism to the Western Hemisphere "would constitute a threat to the sovereignty and political independence of the American states, endangering the peace of America."

As a permanent body of inter-American consultation, the United States together with all the Latin American republics founded the Organization of American States (OAS) in 1948. The Charter of the OAS proclaims the equality of its twenty-one members and lays down the principle of nonintervention in their external and internal affairs. In addition, it calls for the pacific settlement of disputes and provides for consultation on all matters of common interest. The organs of the OAS are the Inter-American Conference, meeting every five years; the meeting of foreign ministers, to deal with emergencies; and the Council of the OAS, a permanent hemispheric parliament with headquarters in Washington. The OAS has successfully settled a number of feuds between some of its smaller members but has been less successful in resolving disputes between larger states. The Organization's major tests have come since 1960, as the United States became involved first in disputes with Cuba and then with Panama (see pp. 102–3).

While the United States has been careful to respect the democratic character of the OAS, her preponderant power gives her a unique position among its members. This has been shown in the United Nations, where most of the countries of Latin America have usually followed the lead of their northern ally. In the all-important economic field, however, the United States, in the opinion of many Latin Americans, has not done as much as she should to justify her leadership. These critics point out that America has been giving far more aid to Europe, Asia, and even Africa, than to Latin America. Other criticism has been leveled against United States tariff policy, which restricts the import of certain Latin American raw materials, especially ores. Finally, the fact that the United States at times has supported Latin American dictators has caused resentment among Latin American liberals. In reply to some of these criticisms, the United States has pointed to the almost 10 billion dollars of private funds invested in Latin America and to the yearly exchange of goods valued at more than 6 billion dollars. These figures show that America's interest in the economy of her southern neighbors is far from negligible. Any comparison with Europe, moreover, which is frequently made by Latin Americans, is considered meaningless, since the more highly developed European economy is able to absorb far greater sums than the backward economies of Latin America.

Still, the mounting wave of anti-Americanism in Central and South America finally led the United States to reassess its Latin American policy. Beginning in the last years of the Eisenhower administration, Washington began supporting various long-range development plans, such as "Operation Pan-America." In 1959 the United States made a dramatic gesture by contributing 45 per cent to a new billion-dollar Inter-American Development Bank, and in 1960 Congress authorized an additional 500 million dollars in development funds for Latin America. The high point in America's efforts to aid Latin America came with the launching of the Alliance for Progress by President Kennedy in 1961. The Charter of the Alliance was signed by the members of the Organization of American States, except Cuba, at Punta del Este, Uruguay, in August, 1961. It calls for a cooperative effort on the part of the American republics to accelerate their economic and social development so as to achieve "the maximum levels of well-being, with equal opportunities for all, in democratic societies adapted to their own needs and desires." Among the specific goals of the Alliance were a yearly rate of growth of 2.5 per cent per capita in each country, minimum schooling of six years for all children, improved water supplies, low-cost housing, agrarian reform, and industrialization. The estimated cost of the program was 20 billion dollars for ten years, of which the United States pledged half.

The Alliance for Progress was hailed at its inception as a historic turning point and a major step forward on Latin America's road toward a better life. But that road, it soon turned out, was beset with obstacles and frustrations. The United States did its part by granting the funds it had promised; but few countries were able to live up to the conditions that would make them eligible for outside aid. President Kennedy had insisted on "self-help and domestic reform" and had called for careful economic planning as prerequisites for any successful development. But such planning required trained experts, who were scarce in Latin America. The potentially most important country, Brazil, was prevented by political instability from participating in the Alliance program. Elsewhere strongly entrenched oligarchies resisted the economic and land reforms needed "to end those conditions which benefit the few at the expense of the needs and dignity of the many." Some advances were made in economic development and social reform. But these fell far short of expectations. Nevertheless, the goals of the Alliance for Progress and the methods it set forth to achieve these goals still offer the best hope for a sound and stable future in Latin America.

TWO TROUBLE SPOTS:
CUBA AND PANAMA

America's increased concern over Latin America coincided with and was influenced by events in Cuba. On January 1, 1959, the rebel forces of Fidel Castro, after more than two years of guerilla fighting, ousted the corrupt and repressive regime of Cuban dictator Fulgencio Batista. Castro's program called for agrarian reform, industrialization, and a far-reaching public works program. It had strong socialist overtones and to some observers smacked of communism. But Castro and his followers asserted that their revolution was "humanist and not Communist." By mid-1960 large sections of Cuba's agriculture and much of her industry had been nationalized, generally without compensation to the former owners. Cubans who did not like these drastic changes were silenced or went into exile. Castro's most ardent supporters came from among the students and the poor. A general election which he had promised before he took power was never held. Instead, Castro emerged as a dictator—the "maximum leader"—backed by a United Party of the Socialist Revolution (PURS). Cuba had exchanged one kind of dictator for another.

In his domestic program Castro achieved some initial successes. The educational system was broadened to eradicate illiteracy and make Cubans more receptive to indoctrination. Improved social services and housing benefited primarily the poorest segment of the population, as did wage increases. When it came to improving the country's economy, however, the Castro regime soon ran into trouble. A four-year development program calling for a 10 per cent annual growth in the gross national product actually brought the reverse. Production of sugar, Cuba's principal source of income, dropped almost 50 per cent between 1961 and 1963, and there were similar declines in other commodities. By 1963 food and consumer goods had to be rationed. The reasons for these reversals were several—poor weather, faulty planning, decline of trade with the free world (especially the United States), and loss of talent through exile of political opponents. To remedy the situation, Cuba turned increasingly toward the Communist bloc, signing a number of trade agreements with Russia and Red China. The initial drive for industrialization was abandoned in 1963, the main emphasis once again being placed on agriculture and sugar.

Castro's alignment with communism began shortly after he took power, although he did not openly proclaim his belief in Marxism-Leninism until late in 1961. Some of his closest associates —his brother Raul and Ernesto ("Che") Guevara—had strong Communist affiliations, and Communists were given important positions in the government. Here they supplied the necessary ideology and experience for the socialist state Castro aimed to create. In time some differences arose between the old-line Communists of Cuba's Communist Party (PSP) and the more recently converted "new" Communists of Castro's inner circle. But these differences do not affect the basically Communist nature and policy of the Cuban state.

Castro's relations with the Soviet Union likewise go back to the early days of the new regime. The first Cuban trade agreement with Russia was signed in February, 1960. It was followed by still closer ties, as mounting attacks against the United States led the latter to reduce and finally, in December, 1960, to eliminate its imports of Cuban sugar. Meanwhile Communist bloc armaments were beginning to arrive in Cuba, and Premier Khrushchev threatened to launch intercontinental missiles against the United States if it intervened in Cuba. The failure of the United States-organized invasion in April, 1961, further encouraged the Russians in their attempts to convert Cuba into a Communist stronghold in the Western Hemisphere. The build-up of Cuba's defenses with help from Russian jets, missiles, and "technicians" finally led to the "missile crisis" in the early fall of 1962. America's firmness in the face of this provocation caused the Russians to retreat, thus showing Castro the limits to which he could count on Soviet support. Still, in his running attacks on the United States and his growing isolation within Latin America, friendship with Moscow remains an indispensable asset for the Cuban dictator.

Castro's relations with the United States were strained from the start. Appealing to Cuban nationalism by blaming most of

Cuba's economic ills on American "colonialism," the Cuban leader hoped to rally popular support to his radical course. The United States, on the other hand, was alarmed by Castro's growing intimacy with Moscow and his attempts to export his revolution to neighboring parts of Central and South America. Cuba's nationalization program, furthermore, affected American investments totaling close to a billion dollars. Beginning in mid-1960, relations between the two countries changed from tension to hostility, and in January, 1961, the United States broke off diplomatic relations with Cuba. There followed the ill-fated invasion by Cuban exiles of the "Bay of Pigs" in April, 1961. It had the backing of the United States government, and President Kennedy assumed full responsibility for the several miscalculations that led to its failure. The result of the invasion was to strengthen Castro's position in Cuba and to raise his reputation in Latin America. The missile crisis of 1962 undid most of these gains. Since then the Cuban dictator has continued in his Moscow-assigned role as a thorn in America's side. He has periodically asserted Cuba's claim to the United States naval base at Guantánamo Bay, and he continues to foment trouble in other parts of Latin America.

The United States has been careful at every point to obtain Latin American support in its various showdowns with Castro. In August, 1960, the foreign ministers of the Organization of American States, with three abstentions, signed the Declaration of San José, which condemned "intervention . . . from an extracontinental power in the affairs of the American republics" and the acceptance of such intervention by any American power. While the United States interpreted the document as "a clear indictment of the Castro government," some of the other signatories denied such an interpretation. United States efforts to have Cuba expelled from the OAS did not succeed until January, 1962. Even then six nations, representing more than half the area and population of Latin America, abstained from ousting Cuba. A far more solid backing was given the United States at the time of the missile crisis. On October 23, 1962, the Council of the OAS called unanimously for the withdrawal of all offensive weapons from Cuba and authorized the use of armed force, if necessary, to prevent additional weapons from reaching Cuba. There still remained the threat of subversion by Castro's agents and sympathizers elsewhere in Latin America. Several countries, notably Chile, Mexico, Uruguay, and Bolivia, opposed OAS action on this point. The issue of

Cuban subversion became acute in the fall of 1963, when Castro supported pro-Communist guerillas and terrorists in Venezuela in their efforts to prevent re-election of a moderate democratic government. Venezuela's protests to the OAS led to a resolution by that body in July, 1964, condemning Cuba as an aggressor and providing for economic and diplomatic sanctions against her. The four countries mentioned above did not vote for the resolution.

The Organization of American States also played an important role as mediator in another conflict between the United States and a small Latin American nation—Panama. There have been several anti-United States demonstrations in Panama in recent years. The most serious of these occurred in January, 1964, when a clash between Panamanian demonstrators and United States troops along the Canal Zone left several dead on both sides. In the ensuing crisis Panama broke off diplomatic relations with the United States and demanded revision of the 1903 treaty which gave the United States the right "in perpetuity" to construct, operate, and maintain a canal across the Isthmus of Panama. Washington was ready to discuss some specific requests for a larger Panamanian share in the Canal's profits or for larger participation of Panamanians in its operation. But the Johnson administration stood firm in its refusal to renegotiate the basic provisions of the canal treaty. As tempers rose on both sides, the OAS Council set a precedent by invoking its peace-keeping machinery for the first time in a dispute involving the United States. Serving as mediators rather than judges, the foreign ministers of the American states recommended that the two governments re-establish diplomatic relations and appoint special ambassadors to negotiate their differences. This was done in April, 1964, and discussions between the United States and Panama were started in May. The readiness of the United States to refrain from unilateral action in dealing with the trouble spots in Panama and Cuba went a long way toward dispelling the suspicions which the Nations of Latin America had long harbored against the "colossus of the north." To maintain and strengthen the spirit of partnership within the Organization of American States and the Alliance for Progress remains a major task of United States foreign policy.

4

THE WINNERS

Alexei N. Kosygin (1.) and Leonid I. Brezhnev (r.)
who, on October 16, 1964, succeeded Nikita S. Khrushchev
as heads of the Soviet government and Communist
Party respectively. WIDE WORLD PHOTOS.

THE SOVIET UNION
AND ITS
SATELLITES

THE MOST IMPORTANT SINGLE EVENT IN
Russian history since World War II was the death of Premier
Stalin on March 5, 1953. The passing of this most powerful dictator
of modern times marked the end of an era. It was under Stalin
that Russian communism made the most headway in pursuit of its
major aims: to make the Soviet Union the strongest nation on
earth and to extend the influence of communism over as wide an
area as possible. More than any other individual, with the possible
exception of Hitler, this forbidding man was responsible for the
divided and insecure world in which we live.

RUSSIA UNDER STALIN

Joseph Stalin gave his name to a particularly rigid and orthodox
type of communism. Politically Stalinism brought to perfection

the dictatorship of one party, and ultimately of one man, over a country of two hundred million people, using every means of control, from censorship to mass executions and slave labor, to reach its totalitarian goals. Economically Stalinism carried out nothing less than an industrial and agricultural revolution. Within one generation the Soviet Union was transformed into one of the world's leading industrial powers, at the same time increasing its agricultural efficiency and output through large-scale collective farming. In the field of foreign affairs Stalin prior to World War II adhered to his policy of assuring first the victory of "socialism in one country," that is, Russia. He thus abstained, temporarily, from pursuing the fundamental aim of Soviet policy: the elimination of capitalism and the promotion of world revolution. During World War II the government's ambitious schemes of economic development were interrupted. But once the fighting was over, Stalinism continued where it had left off, becoming, if anything, more rigid at home and changing from a policy of isolationism in foreign affairs to one of territorial and ideological expansion.

In 1946 the first general elections since 1937 for the Supreme Soviet, the highest "legislative" authority in the U.S.S.R., produced the expected results. More than 99 per cent of the eligible voters endorsed the official list of Communist candidates. Membership in the Communist Party, which, under more liberal admission requirements during the war, had almost reached the six million mark, was now again subjected to closer scrutiny, resulting in large-scale expulsions. The executive powers of the Soviet government continued to be vested in a Council of Ministers (prior to 1946 called Council of People's Commissars), with Stalin serving as Chairman or Premier. But the real power, as in the past, rested with the Communist Party, its Central Committee, its eleven-member Politburo (since 1952 called Presidium), and its First Secretary, Joseph Stalin. The relationship between party and government has been compared to that existing between the board of directors and the managers of a large corporation, with most of the leading figures occupying corresponding positions of influence in both government and party. As for the relative standing of each individual within the Soviet hierarchy, the outside world depended for its information chiefly on whatever conclusions it wanted to draw from the lineup of Soviet dignitaries at official functions. Physical proximity to Stalin at such functions was usually interpreted as a sign of influence. Occasional changes were made in the Soviet hierarchy, such as the replacement in 1949 of Foreign Minister Vyacheslav M. Molotov by Andrei Vyshinsky, and of Defense Minister Nikolai A. Bulganin by Alexander Vasilevsky, and the appointment of Georgi M. Malenkov to succeed the party's leading ideologist, Andrei Zhdanov, who had died in 1948. Any such change usually led to speculation abroad as to the possible line of succession in case of Stalin's death. Yet the inner workings of the Soviet system continued to remain a deep mystery to outsiders.

There were other changes during the postwar era, mostly in the direction of greater orthodoxy, both in the Marxian and in the traditional Russian sense. Leading writers, artists, and scientists were accused by the Central Committee of the Communist Party of having lost touch with the masses by showing bourgeois influences in their work. The persons thus charged were forced to confess and recant their "errors." The Russian people, who had always been kept from contact with the West, now were isolated more than ever. They were indoctrinated with a nationalistic view of their country's past and present in which Russia emerged as the inventor and originator of all good things and Stalin as the greatest of national leaders and the father of his country. With this emphasis on Russian nationalism went a relaxation in the government's antireligious policy. Already during the war the Kremlin, recognizing the continued strength of religious feeling among the Russian people, had sanctioned the election of a new patriarch for the Orthodox Church. At the end of the war the government had restored half of the religious property that had been confiscated in the past. The Church repaid these concessions by abandoning its opposition to the Communist regime and welcoming the government's policy of once again recognizing the institution of the family as the foundation of national life.

Stalin's most significant contribution was in the economic sphere, where "he found Russia working with the wooden plough and left her equipped with atomic piles." No country ever experienced an industrial revolution as rapidly and against such terrific odds as did the Soviet Union. Today she ranks second among the world's industrial nations, and hopes to catch up with and ultimately surpass the United States. Russia's industrial revolution was carried on through state planning rather than private initiative, and was pursued with a cold-blooded ruthlessness that has had no parallel, except in the recent history of Communist China.

Partly as a result of purges but mostly from periodic famines, millions of Russians died so that "socialism in one country" could become a reality. Large-scale industrialization did not begin in earnest until the launching of the first Five-Year Plan in 1928. After ten years it had made sufficient strides so that the third Five-Year Plan, which was put into effect in 1938, for the first time permitted an increase in the production of consumer goods. Prior to this time the emphasis had been on heavy industry. But just as the Russian people, after years of sacrifice, were about to taste some of the fruits of their labor, the war intervened.

It is difficult to get a clear picture of the economic effects of the war. Russia's losses were staggering, heavier than those of all the other Allied powers combined. But the Russians had already begun reconstruction while the war was still in progress. They had shifted many of their major industries to regions beyond the reach of the German invaders, using the generous assistance of American Lend-Lease funds to make possible this relocation. Soviet recovery after the war certainly would have been less rapid had the situation been as dismal as Soviet leaders, in their claims for large reparations, asserted. The task before the Soviet government in 1945 was twofold: to repair the damages of war and to continue the prewar process of industrialization. To achieve these aims, the fourth Five-Year Plan was launched in 1946. It was completed in 1950, with results that supposedly exceeded its original goals. Even if due allowance is made for the exaggeration of official Soviet statistics, the achievements of Russia's postwar economic development were remarkable. Production of coal, steel, electric power, and oil all showed substantial increases over prewar levels, and the total output of the Soviet Union in the early 1950's was getting close to the combined productions of the three major nations of western Europe: Great Britain, France and Germany. These gains were made possible only at the cost of great personal sacrifices on the part of the Russian people. Through a drastic currency devaluation in 1947 they lost most of their savings and had to work harder and longer to eke out a minimum existence. Consumer goods continued to be scarce, as a fifth Five-Year Plan, to be completed by 1955, called for further increases in heavy industry, notably the production of steel.

Compared to the rapid growth of Russian industry under Stalin, developments in agriculture were far less impressive. While industrial production between 1940 and 1952 almost doubled, agricultural output during the same period increased by only 10 per cent. The main features of Stalin's agrarian policy were collectivization (consolidation of individual holdings into large collective farms) and mechanization. Neither of these innovations appealed to the backward and conservative Russian peasant, who tried to resist the government's policy by every possible means. Resistance was met by reprisals, without markedly improving the situation. One of the main grievances of the peasantry was its inability to buy an equivalent in consumer goods for the foodstuffs it was asked to surrender. Just before World War II agrarian unrest had somewhat decreased, as peasants were permitted to cultivate small individual plots of an acre or less for their own use, free from state control. But once the war was over, the government again stepped up collectivization, not merely by extending it to regions recently annexed—such as the Baltic states—but also by merging the already existing collective farms into still larger supercollectives. The government was aided in its control over agriculture by a state-owned system of machine-tractor stations, which supplied the necessary mechanization for large-scale farming.

EASTERN EUROPE UNDER STALIN

The main events of Russia's foreign policy under Stalin are discussed elsewhere in this book (see Chapter 1). Whether proceeding by plan or pushed by events, Stalin after 1945 abandoned his earlier policy of isolationism. He took full advantage of the opportunities presented by the initial confusion of the postwar era to advance the fortunes of the Soviet Union and of world communism. These two aims have motivated Soviet policy from its beginnings. It is only in the methods used to realize these aims that we find the wide variety of attitudes, from aggressiveness to agreeableness, that characterize Russian policy at different times. With their belief in the inevitability of a Communist victory, Russia's leaders can afford to be patient; and with their strong hold over their own people and over most Communists outside Russia, they can afford to be opportunistic, adjusting their policy to changing circumstances. Perseverance in long-range aims combined with expediency in short-range methods were the characteristics not only of Stalin and the men who ruled Russia before him but also of the men who succeeded him.

111

We have already noted the westward expansion of Soviet influence during the years immediately following World War II. Russia annexed outright some 185,000 square miles with nearly 25 million people, and she gained indirect control over another 560,000 square miles inhabited by almost 100 million. The Soviet Union was thus able to remake most of eastern Europe, with the exception of Finland, after its own image. This transformation was facilitated by a number of factors: the blindness of the Western Allies to Russia's ultimate aims, the actual occupation of the region by Russian troops, and the political and economic weaknesses of an area that already twice in our century had embroiled the world in a major war. In 1945 the nations of eastern Europe were exhausted by the heavy sacrifices of war and German occupation; they were divided by age-old nationalist rivalries; and they were disillusioned by the past failures of their governments, many of which had become Fascist dictatorships even before Hitler. Thus, the nations of eastern Europe presented the kind of political and spiritual vacuum that seems particularly favorable to the spread of communism.

A further factor aiding the communization of eastern Europe was the manner in which the transition from liberal regimes to "people's democracies" was brought about. With minor variations, developments in the eight states thus affected—Albania, Bulgaria, Czechoslovakia, East Germany, Hungary, Poland, Romania, and Yugoslavia—followed a common pattern. As a first step the Soviet occupation authorities sponsored the formation of coalition or "united front" governments made up of representatives from those groups that had opposed the Nazis during the war. The outward appearance of democracy was thus maintained, chiefly for the benefit of the West. Yet the Communist contingents of such coalitions, notably in Yugoslavia, Poland, and Albania, played a dominant role from the very start. By holding key positions, such as the ministries of interior and justice, and enjoying the support of the Russians, the Communists were able to consolidate their power. This power they used to suppress right-wing opposition groups and to initiate the first moves toward nationalization of industry and collectivization of agriculture. As soon as they felt sufficiently strong, the Communists proceeded to the second and more difficult step in their seizure of power. This was the gradual ousting, by threats or on trumped-up charges of treason, of their non-Communist coalition partners. The method and timing used differed with each country. In Yugoslavia and Albania the Communists had absolute authority from the very beginning. In Bulgaria and Romania the non-Communists gave way by the middle of 1945, in East Germany by early 1946, in Poland and Hungary during the first half of 1947, and in Czechoslovakia, as we have seen, not until early 1948.

In all these countries, with the exception of Czechoslovakia, the absence of a strong democratic tradition further facilitated communization. The only groups at all capable of putting up any opposition, and therefore the main targets of Communist attacks, were the agrarian socialist movements in the various countries. But despite the fact that they commanded a far greater following than their Communist partners, the agrarian socialists proved no match for the Communists and their skill at conquest by infiltration. Some agrarian leaders were allowed to go into exile. Others were able to escape. These fortunate ones became active abroad in organizations devoted to the future liberation of their homelands and helped to form in 1954 the Assembly of Captive European Nations (ACEN). As for the rest of the agrarian leaders, they were either jailed or executed on fabricated charges of espionage, treason, or sabotage. Another potential opposition force, the Catholic Church, strongly entrenched in such countries as Poland, Czechoslovakia, Hungary, and Yugoslavia, was similarly dealt with. Leading religious figures, like Cardinal Mindszenty of Hungary, Cardinal Wyszynski of Poland, and Archbishop (later Cardinal) Stepinac of Yugoslavia, were imprisoned on alleged charges of treason. Possessions of the churches were nationalized, and the minor clergy were deprived of all influence.

The victory of communism in eastern Europe was virtually complete by early 1948. Politically, one-party rule now prevailed in all the "people's democracies," despite the nominal existence of some of the former coalition parties. As in the Soviet Union, central committees of the Communist Party made all major political decisions and appointed all important officials, usually following instructions from Moscow. Like prerevolutionary Russia, most of eastern Europe, with the exception of Czechoslovakia, was predominantly agrarian. Again as in Russia, one of the major aims of the new regimes everywhere was to improve their backward agricultural economies through increased industrialization. There were various five- or six-year plans, and in Bulgaria industry actually began overtaking agriculture. Czechoslovakia, the only country already highly industrialized in the past, played a key role in aiding the industrialization of her neighbors and in supplying arms to the Eastern satellites. The Polish Six-Year Plan covering the years 1950–55 aimed at an increase of 154 per cent in heavy industry and only 11 per cent in consumer goods. This emphasis on heavy industry was also noticeable in most other countries of the Soviet bloc, resulting in the same low standard of living as in the Soviet Union. In the agricultural field the emphasis again, as in Russia, was on forced collectivization, with widely differing results. There was considerable opposition among farmers and workers to the economic policy of their new Communist masters. Efforts at resistance were shown in absenteeism and slowdowns, but also in occasional riots, such as those in Czechoslovakia and East Germany in 1953. Such discontent was suppressed ruthlessly.

Aside from introducing their own type of government and economy, the Russians were careful to maintain as close a hold as possible over their puppet states by means of ideological, military, and economic agreements. We have already discussed the formation of the Cominform, the signing of various mutual assistance pacts, and the inauguration of the so-called Molotov Plan via the Council for Mutual Economic Assistance or COMECON (see Chapter 1). The general effect of these agreements was to integrate the satellite countries with each other and with the Soviet Union and to insure their maximum usefulness to the latter. To bolster Eastern military strength, the nations of the Soviet orbit were forced to maintain armed forces far beyond their means and exceeding the terms of the peace treaties signed in 1947.

Two countries in eastern Europe, East Germany and Yugoslavia, deserve special mention. The first is not really a nation at all, but only a part of one. We have already traced the gradual division of Germany in the early years of the cold war. The German Democratic Republic, as East Germany is called in the Communist world, was officially established in October, 1949. Its government, which thus far has not been recognized by either West Germany or the Western Allies, is dominated by the Socialist Unity Party (SED). Other more moderate parties continue a shadowy existence but wield no real influence. President of the republic until his death in 1960 was veteran Communist Wilhelm Pieck. The post of Minister President was first held by ex-Socialist Otto Grotewohl, who died in 1964 and was succeeded by Communist Willi Stoph. The most powerful figure in East Germany, however, is Walter Ulbricht, Communist leader of the SED. In

1960 Ulbricht became chairman of a new Council of State, which took over the functions of the presidency. In most essential respects the German Democratic Republic followed the course of the other "people's democracies." Most of its industries were nationalized, and despite various handicaps and shortages, industrial production by 1954 had risen almost 80 per cent above the 1936 level. Agriculture fared less well, due to a haphazard land reform immediately after the war which divided the more efficiently run large estates among peasant proprietors. Attempts at collectivization, begun in 1948, did not prove very successful. Even though the region had always been among the most productive in Germany, it did not grow sufficient food, and large quantities had to be imported. The standard of living of the East Germans, consequently, remained far below that of their western brethren. Popular discontent with this state of affairs found release in a steady flow of refugees, mostly farmers, into the western Federal Republic. A series of riots in several East German cities, including East Berlin, on June 17, 1953, was put down by Soviet occupation forces. Matters were made worse by Russia's strict policy toward her occupation zone during the Stalin era. As a major source of reparations, the eastern republic was forced to pay far more than the 10 billion dollars originally demanded by the Soviet Union. When reparations were officially discontinued in 1953, the drain on East Germany's economy continued, as the Germans had to buy back those industrial enterprises that had been confiscated by the Soviets right after the war.

The case of Yugoslavia was quite different. While everywhere else in eastern Europe the Russians were tightening their hold, Yugoslavia alone was able to free herself from Soviet control. The Communist forces of Josip Broz, better known as Marshal Tito, having played a major role in liberating their country from the Axis, had from the beginning been far less dependent on Russian support than the Communist minorities elsewhere. Yugoslavia thus remained relatively free from Russian interference. Still, in her internal developments, Yugoslavia at first followed closely the pattern found in the other satellites. Tito set up a "people's republic" in 1945, with a constitution closely resembling that of the U.S.S.R. Moderate opponents, such as General Mihailovich, were purged. The nation also embarked on a Five-Year Plan of industrial development and initiated a drive to collectivize agriculture. Outwardly relations between Belgrade and Moscow appeared friendly, and until 1948 Yugoslavia was generally looked upon as firmly within the Russian orbit.

As we now know, differences between Tito and Stalin had begun to arise as early as 1945. The first disagreement came over the question of Trieste, where Tito felt he did not receive adequate Russian support. Discord ultimately extended to other fields, as the self-assured and able Yugoslav dictator made it plain that he intended to be master in his own house. The open break came in the spring of 1948, as the Russians first recalled their military and technical advisers, and then had Tito and his party expelled from the Cominform for doctrinal errors and hostility to the Soviet Union. This action was followed by a severing of all economic and military ties between the Russian bloc and its onetime member.

The break with Moscow, greeted in the West as a major Russian setback, did not at first bring any change in Yugoslavia's domestic policy. Tito remained a Communist, although his ideology of national communism, or "Titoism," differed from the orthodox Stalinist line. In foreign affairs, on the other hand, the Yugoslav leader gradually moved closer to the West, not only economically, by concluding a series of agreements providing economic aid to Yugoslavia, but also politically. Tito opposed Chinese intervention in Korea, resumed diplomatic relations with Greece, and improved relations with Italy, which ultimately resulted in a settlement of the controversy over Trieste. Beginning in 1950 there also were signs of a certain liberalization in Yugoslavia's policy at home. Control over heavy industry and farming was decentralized. More than four-fifths of the collective farms were dissolved, and participation in collectivization was made voluntary. A system of "workers' management" was adopted in industry, and production was put on a profit basis. The institution of political commissars was abolished, and the Communist Party henceforth was to rely on persuasion rather than compulsion. In addition, freedom of worship was granted, the secret ballot was introduced, and women were given the vote. In January, 1953, the Soviet-style constitution was revised in the direction of greater decentralization with a parliament of two chambers (a Federal Council and a Council of Producers) and a president (Marshal Tito). To strengthen her defenses, Yugoslavia in February, 1953, joined Turkey and Greece in a treaty of friendship (Treaty of Ankara), supplemented the following year by a military alliance (Bled Alliance). In addition, military funds and equipment from the Western powers, especially the United States, were extended to Yugoslavia beginning in 1951.

From all these changes it seemed quite clear that the break between Tito and Stalin was complete. Stalin feared that Yugoslavia's desertion might find imitators among the other satellites. He therefore used his influence over the Cominform to start a general purge of any Communist leaders who showed the slightest signs of independence. The resulting imprisonment or execution of a number of Communist stalwarts in Bulgaria, Hungary, Czechoslovakia, Poland, and Romania prevented any further defections and insured continued blind obedience among satellite Communists. At the same time Stalin laid plans for a major purge at home to consolidate his absolute power by ridding himself of any possible rivals among his lieutenants. It was at this critical point that the Russian leader died, leaving his country to the very men he had been about to destroy.

"COLLECTIVE LEADERSHIP"

Contrary to expectations of many observers abroad, the death of Stalin did not unleash a struggle for his succession. Since there was no single individual strong enough to assume all of Stalin's vast powers, responsibility was divided among a group of his closest associates. Georgi M. Malenkov was appointed premier; Lavrenti P. Beria continued as chief of the all-powerful secret police; Vyacheslav M. Molotov was again placed in charge of foreign affairs; and Marshal Nikolai A. Bulganin was made minister of defense, with Marshal Georgi K. Zhukov as his assistant. A little later another important appointment made Nikita S. Khrushchev First Secretary of the Communist Party's Central Committee. This was the post from which Stalin had risen almost thirty years before to become dictator of the Soviet Union.

From all these changes it appeared as though one-man rule in Russia had been replaced by "collective leadership." Again there were Western observers who predicted that this state of affairs could not last and that Stalin's heirs would soon start quarreling among themselves. These expectations seemed to come true when, less than four months after Stalin's death, Beria was expelled from the party for "criminal anti-party and anti-government activities," was arrested, and was executed. But the purge, in its violent

117

form at least, stopped with Beria and some of his associates. The new regime now settled down to a policy at home and abroad that appeared to be a radical break with the Stalinist past.

As a start, the new Soviet leaders decreed a far-reaching amnesty of political prisoners. This was followed by promises of reform in the administration of justice, the methods of the secret police, and the running of the "corrective" (that is, slave) labor camps. Of still greater interest to the average Soviet citizen were the announcements that a shift toward greater production of consumer goods was being contemplated. To appeal to the agrarian segment, government control of collective farming was relaxed, and renewed encouragement was given to the cultivation of small individual plots. In addition, agricultural taxation was lowered, some delivery quotas were reduced, and government payments for produce delivered by collective farms were raised. Still more startling to the outside world than these signs of relaxation at home were the pronouncements on foreign policy made by Russia's new leaders. "There is not one disputed and undecided question," Premier Malenkov said in his inaugural address to the Supreme Soviet, "that cannot be decided by peaceful means on the basis of the mutual understanding of interested countries. This is our attitude toward all states, among them the United States of America." This was a new kind of language for the Kremlin to use. And it was not long before words were followed by deeds. In the summer of 1953 the Soviet Union aided, or at least did not prevent, the signing of an armistice in Korea; a year later the fighting in Indochina was stopped; and in 1955 peace was at long last concluded with Austria.

The most obvious explanation for Russia's new policy of concessions at home and abroad was that it facilitated the transition from one regime to the next by easing tension and calming fears. During 1954 there were already signs that the influence of Malenkov was declining, while Khrushchev was gradually emerging as the party's official spokesman. Late in 1954 an editorial in *Pravda* again favored Stalin's emphasis on heavy industry as the basis of Soviet economic and military might. The climax of what must have been a major internal struggle came on February 8, 1955, when Malenkov asked the Supreme Soviet to relieve him of his duties as premier on grounds of incompetence. In particular, he admitted responsibility for errors in agricultural policy, a field with which his rival Khrushchev had been equally, if not more, concerned. Whatever the real causes, the result of the crisis was that Defense Minister Bulganin, upon Khrushchev's recommendation, was appointed Malenkov's successor, with Marshal Zhukov assuming the post vacated by Bulganin. Malenkov, however, was neither exiled nor executed but was merely given a less important position, at the same time maintaining his membership in the Presidium of the Central Committee, the small clique that rules the Soviet Union. Apparently, even in its internal shakeups, the Soviet government had adopted a "new look."

The ouster of Malenkov was a major step forward in the steady rise to power of Nikita S. Khrushchev. Using his influence with the party's rank and file, this shrewd politician within the next three years managed to push aside one after another of his colleagues until in 1958 he emerged as the virtual successor to Stalin. The first to go after Malenkov was Molotov, who was removed as foreign minister in 1956. Shortly thereafter riots in Poland and a revolution in Hungary gave rise to dissatisfaction among the members of the Presidium with Khrushchev's policy. In June, 1957, a majority of the Presidium decided to challenge their powerful comrade. But it was already too late. Appealing to the Central Committee over the heads of the Presidium, Khrushchev succeeded in ousting the leaders of the opposition, among them Malenkov and Molotov, and in substituting a number of his own supporters. Khrushchev's maneuver was made possible because he had the support of the army, in the person of Defense Minister Zhukov, who now also became a member of the Presidium. But his political role was short-lived. Fearing Zhukov as a possible rival, Khrushchev in October, 1957, had him removed both from his post as minister and from the Presidium. The final victory of Khrushchev came in March, 1958, when he replaced Bulganin as premier, thus combining the two positions of party and government chiefs which Stalin had held before him.

This was the end of "collective leadership." Like Stalin, Khrushchev now was the acknowledged leader of the Soviet Union and as such the object of adulation at home and of admiration or animosity abroad. He was the public advocate of any major change in his government's policy, supreme arbiter in domestic disputes, and chief voice in Soviet foreign policy. But there were some important differences from the days of Stalin. Russia was no longer a police state run by terror and according to the whims of a paranoid individual. It had become a complex bureaucratic dictatorship, administered as rationally and efficiently as its vast size and the character of its people permit. A single individual like Khrushchev could no more hope to manage this gigantic bureaucratic machine than the president of a large corporation can hope to run his enterprise without the assistance of top executives and trained subordinates. The executives and managers in the Soviet Union are supplied by the Communist Party. It is in the party, therefore, that final authority rests. Khrushchev, as head of the party, had a decisive voice in selecting his lieutenants. But the fact remained that he needed a group of key men to help him run the Soviet Union. Among the leading figures next to Khrushchev, the most influential were Anastas I. Mikoyan, one of the few remaining Old Bolsheviks and since 1964 Chairman of the Supreme Soviet, that is, president of the Soviet Union; Leonid I. Brezhnev, deputy to Khrushchev in the Secretariat of the Communist Party's Central Committee; and Nikolai V. Podgorny, Mikhail A. Suslov, and Alexei N. Kosygin, all of them members of the Central Committee's Presidium or its Secretariat. It was this group that asserted itself in October, 1964, and, by ousting Khrushchev from his apparent one-man rule, reinstituted a measure of "collective leadership" (see p. 204).

THE KHRUSHCHEV ERA

The most striking feature of Soviet domestic policy since Stalin has been the abandonment of terror as an instrument of government. Ever since the execution of Beria the arbitrary use of force has been de-emphasized, police tribunals have been superseded by regular courts, and slave labor camps no longer are the symbol of Russian communism. The high point of this retreat from terror came in a blistering attack on Stalin by Khrushchev during the Twentieth Congress of the Communist Party in Moscow in 1956. For four hours the First Secretary of the party denounced the dead dictator, accusing Stalin of excessive self-glorification and the abuse of power and charging him with the deaths of "many thousands of honest and innocent Communists." Stalin, Khrushchev said, had been "a very distrustful man, sickly suspicious," and had become more so toward the end of his life. Even Stalin's conduct of the war, usually considered one of his great contributions, came under fire for the insufficient preparation of Soviet defenses and the unnecessary sacrifice of hundreds of thousands of Russian lives. Communist history, Khrushchev concluded, had been so deliberately twisted to satisfy Stalin's desire for praise that it needed to be "thoroughly revised."

The world was puzzled by this washing of Russia's dirty linen in public. If Khrushchev's speech helped to dissociate the new Soviet regime from its predecessor, it did so at the price of causing confusion in Communist ranks and giving ammunition to Russia's opponents abroad. To be sure, the new Russian leader afterwards modified his stand and admitted that Stalin's errors had been justified at the time by the need "to safeguard the gains of the revolution." Still, the effect of the tirade against Stalin within Russia was such as to make any return to the repressive practices of the Stalin era difficult, if not impossible.

Not only did Khrushchev give the Russian people freedom from fear, at least as long as they remained loyal Communists, he also gave them many other things the majority of them had never known. "When you have a hungry stomach," he once said in the jovial manner he affected, "it is sometimes very difficult to understand the theory of Marxism-Leninism. But if you can have a nice apartment and good food as well as cultural achievements, then surely everyone must say: 'Certainly I'm for Communism.'" The Soviet Union today is still far removed from the Marxian ideal of a classless society. There is a wide gulf between the upper class—party secretaries, high-ranking bureaucrats, factory and farm managers, leading scientists, and the like—and the mass of workers and peasants. But Russia's leaders now seem to be aware of the benefits to be derived from giving their people some share in the nation's wealth. The result has been a series of measures aimed at mitigating the more glaring differences in income and privileges: a minimum wage has been set; social security benefits have been raised; secondary schooling has been extended; and production of consumer goods has been stepped up. In agriculture, emphasis has been on increased production of meat and dairy products, where Russia had been deficient in the past. Under the current Seven-Year Plan, the Russian people have been promised not only necessities like new housing, but amenities like refrigerators and television sets. A start has even been made in reducing work hours, with the five-day week as the ultimate aim.

The liberalization of Russian life has also spread to the intellectual and cultural sphere. Where under Stalin criticism of government policy was synonymous with treason, such criticism is now permitted, as long as it does not attack basic Communist concepts. The fact that all information media are government-controlled, of course, keeps any unorthodox views from being spread. In the artistic field "socialist realism" is still the official style; but "modernism," hitherto tabu, is now tolerated. Soviet writers in recent years have taken advantage of the new freedom to criticize or satirize the Soviet system. Some authors, like Ilya Ehrenburg and Vladimir Dudintsev, have been frowned upon for their outspokenness, and others, notably Boris Pasternak, were officially reprimanded and denied permission to publish some of their works in the Soviet Union. But none of them were given the punishment they would have received under Stalin.

The effects of the "thaw" in Soviet domestic affairs—and there have been other manifestations of it, such as the opportunity Russians now have of learning about Western culture—has been to awaken a spirit of loyalty and initiative among the Russian people that had been absent under the Stalinist system of strict obedience based on fear. The government under Khrushchev made a conscious effort to encourage this initiative, especially in the economic sphere. In the past Russia's economic administration had been highly centralized, all decisions being made by various ministries in Moscow and handed down through a vast and cumbersome bureaucratic hierarchy. This practice was abandoned by Khrushchev. Instead regional economic councils now supervise most of the enterprises in a given area, except those requiring centralized administration. The managers of individual industries and collective farms have been given greater freedom and responsibility, in the hope that individual initiative, combined with state planning, will make for increased efficiency and insure the economic progress which is the overriding aim of Soviet policy.

Russia's economic goals are for the Communist bloc to outproduce the free world and for the Soviet Union to outproduce the United States. In the opinion of some Western observers these goals, while improbable, are not impossible. Russia has mineral resources far exceeding those of the United States, she has a labor force better disciplined than that of any country and better educated today than at any time in Russian history; and she has the technological know-how—as proved by her achievements in the space and missile fields—to make full use of automation and other revolutionary production methods. On the other hand there are also certain obstacles to Russian progress. Her labor supply has been seriously affected by the reduced birth rate due to World War II, and most workers are still living in European Russia, rather than in the mineral-rich Urals. Russia's capital resources, furthermore, while huge, are not considered sufficient for the vast expansion program contemplated, especially as large funds are needed for defense, space exploration, housing, and other nonproductive projects. And, finally, the perennial issue of consumer goods versus heavy industry has by no means been resolved. For the time being the Russian government adheres to its slogan "heavy industry first." But in 1963 Khrushchev also launched a multi-billion-dollar expansion program for Russia's chemical industry which has lagged far behind in development. The production of fertilizers, insecticides, plastics, and artificial fibers is ultimately intended to help raise the standard of living of the Russian people, which is still far below that of the West.

While Russia's industrial production has grown by more than 300 per cent since Stalin's death, her agriculture continues to be the major headache it has always been. Farming was the special concern of Premier Khrushchev, and for the first few years after 1953 considerable improvements were noted. Beginning in 1954 Khrushchev sponsored a program to open up vast areas of virgin soil in Kazakhstan, second largest of the fifteen Soviet republics, and in other parts of Central Asia and Siberia. Despite some reversals, the experiment proved successful. Another of Khrushchev's innovations was increased emphasis on feed-grain production, especially corn, to boost the output of meat. In these and other respects he drew freely on the advice and example of American farm experts. The basic solution to the farm problem in Russia continued to be sought through collectivization on an ever larger scale, combined with greater independence for each individual collective. In 1958 the machine-tractor stations were discontinued and their equipment sold to the collective farms. To provide greater incentives, the compulsory delivery system was abolished, capital investment in agriculture was stepped up, taxes were lowered, and farm prices were raised. As a result of all these measures, agricultural production between 1953 and 1958 increased by nearly 50 per cent, and 1958 was the best year Soviet agriculture ever had. Since then, however, agricultural output has slowed down again and at times has even declined. In 1963 the Soviet Union had to purchase large quantities of wheat abroad in order to feed its people. Crop failures, reduced agricultural investment, continued restrictions, these and other reasons are cited for the stagnation in Soviet agriculture. More capital investment, renewed incentives through higher prices, and most important, more intensive cultivation with the aid of fertilizers and machinery are seen as the only way to help the Soviet Union's lagging agriculture keep pace with its rapidly increasing industry.

One sphere in which the Soviet Union made considerable headway under Khrushchev was foreign trade. Under Stalin domestic difficulties and red tape interfered with commercial expansion abroad. Since then things have changed. Russia's exports and imports still lag far behind those of the United States and western Europe. Nevertheless, sufficient progress has been made to cause America some concern. Most Soviet trade continues to be within the Communist orbit. But concerted efforts are also being made to increase exchange with the free world, particularly with the underdeveloped countries. Special attention has also been given to boosting Soviet trade with the United States. Khrushchev offered to buy large quantities of American capital goods—machines and machine tools—if the United States would take raw materials in return or extend credit to the U.S.S.R. There are several obstacles to such a scheme, however, foremost among them the Kremlin's refusal, thus far, to settle its World War II Lend-Lease debt with the United States. Trade between the two superpowers has improved lately, as the United States sold large quantities of wheat to the Russians and the two nations signed a consular treaty, but it is doubtful that it will ever reach the several-billion-dollar mark which Khrushchev set as his goal.

SOVIET FOREIGN POLICY UNDER KHRUSHCHEV

Russia's motives for expanding her commercial contacts with the free world were not only economic, but also political. We shall discuss below the details of East-West relations during the last few years (see Chapter 6). The keynote of these relations was the search for some form of "coexistence" between the free and Communist worlds. Khrushchev sounded the coexistence note at the opening session of the same party congress in 1956 at which he launched his attack against Stalin. In his Secretary's report he asserted that Communist strength made a future war between communism and "capitalist imperialism" no longer inevitable. The working people of the world, he said, would "sooner or later" recognize "the advantages that communism holds out" and would effect a peaceful change from capitalism to socialism, that is, communism. Until then the First Secretary advocated "peaceful coexistence." "Indeed," he said, "there are only two ways: either peaceful coexistence or the most devastating war in history. There is no third alternative." Later on during the congress he claimed that the Russians "want to be friends with the United States and to co-operate with it in peace and international security and also in the economic and cultural fields. We propose this with good intentions, without holding a knife behind our backs."

Such statements certainly were a far cry from Stalin's anti-Western and anticapitalist tirades. But since they were soon followed by renewed acts of Communist agitation in the Middle East and by the ruthless intervention of Soviet troops in Hungary, the United States could hardly be blamed for not taking Khrushchev's honeyed words at face value. Instead Washington preferred to adhere to its cold-war strategy of containment. Russia's growing economic might, moreover, soon posed a new challenge to the West. "We say to the leaders of the capitalist states," Khrushchev said in 1959, "let us try out in practice whose system is better, let us compete without war. This is much better than competing in who will produce more arms and who will smash whom. We stand and always will stand for such competition as will help to raise the well-being of the people to a higher level."

Here a new front had been opened in the cold war, a front, moreover, on which the capitalist West had always thought itself superior to the Communist East. At times Russia seemed on the verge of abandoning her economic challenge in favor of more drastic means to force a showdown. But she soon again returned to competitive economic coexistence as the major theme of her foreign policy. By proving that communism is superior to capitalism in assuring the good life for all, Russia hopes to win to her side, and to the side of communism, the as yet uncommitted peoples of the world, whose ultimate allegiance may decide the outcome of the cold war.

REVOLT AMONG THE SATELITES

One of the best ways of testing the sincerity of Russia's peaceful pronouncement on foreign policy was to see what changes, if any, her relations with the satellite nations of eastern Europe would undergo during the Khrushchev era. The "new course" adopted by Stalin's successors in Russia was soon imitated in the satellites. "Collective leadership" became the order of the day; political prisoners were released; there was a shift in emphasis from heavy industry to consumer goods; and collectivization in agriculture was modified or abandoned. A second wave of anti-Stalinism occurred in 1956, following Khrushchev's blast against the architect of the satellite system. None of these actions in any way weakened Moscow's domination over eastern Europe. On the contrary, the Soviet Union in 1955 strengthened its hold by sponsoring the Warsaw Pact of mutual assistance (usually considered the Eastern counterpart of NATO), which united the armed forces of the Soviet bloc under Russian command, and permitted Russia to station troops within the satellite countries. Furthermore, the admission to the United Nations in 1955 of those satellites not yet members (Albania, Bulgaria, Hungary, and Romania) was seen as an indication that the *status quo* in eastern Europe was recognized by the rest of the world. Still, there were some signs of a growing desire among the satellite regimes, if not for complete independence from Soviet control, at least for greater freedom from constant Russian interference.

Such freedom had been won by Marshal Tito of Yugoslavia in 1948, although at the price of being expelled from the Communist family. Since Stalin's death relations between Moscow and Belgrade, chiefly due to Soviet initiative, had improved rapidly. The climax came in 1955 and 1956 as first the Cominform (which had expelled Yugoslavia in 1948) was dissolved, then Foreign Minister Molotov (who had led the fight against Tito) was dismissed, and finally Tito visited Moscow to repay an earlier visit by Khrushchev and Bulganin. At the end of his stay Tito and Bulganin signed an agreement officially renewing relations between their two countries and charting a common course on many important issues of foreign policy. Still more important was a simultaneous declaration by Tito and Khrushchev, in their roles as secretaries of their respective Communist parties, defining the principles that were to govern relations between the Communist parties of sovereign states. Its key sentence declared that "the roads of Socialist development are different in different countries." Here was a belated recognition by the Kremlin of one of the main principles of Titoism: that not all Communist countries need follow blindly the Russian lead and example.

The implications of this Moscow Declaration were not lost upon the satellites who, already restive, now became even more so. In the course of 1956 it became clear that the Soviets were getting worried over the desire for emancipation from Russian rule among their subject peoples. In the fall of the year Khrushchev, in long talks with Tito, tried to find ways of reconciling the spread of Titoism with continued Soviet domination over eastern Europe. At this point, in late October, 1956, events in Poland and Hungary took the initiative out of Russian hands. Both these countries had always been known for their fervent nationalism; both were devoutly Catholic; both harbored a deep-seated hatred of Russia that went back before the advent of communism; and both, under the provisions of the Warsaw Pact, still had to endure the presence of large Soviet garrisons on their soil. The roots of the upheavals that occurred within these two satellites, therefore, were quite similar. Both revolts were motivated by strong nationalist sentiments against the domination of a hated foreign power. In the revolts themselves, however, there were significant differences between Poland and Hungary. These differences were mainly responsible for the success of rebellion in the one and its failure in the other.

Events in Poland grew largely out of the general relaxation of Communist rule that had taken place there in the early months of 1956. Workers' riots in the industrial region of Poznan in June of that year were put down with the usual harshness, but, by Communist standards, the trial of the surviving rioters was fair and the verdict moderate. One of Poland's leading Communists, Wladyslaw Gomulka, who had been purged on charges of Titoism in 1948, had been rehabilitated in the spring of 1956. But Gomulka refused to rejoin the government as long as Soviet Marshal Konstantin Rokossovsky remained Polish defense minister and a member of Poland's Politburo. In October, 1956, despite the intervention of Khrushchev and Molotov, Gomulka had his way:

the Politburo elected him secretary and ousted Rokossovsky. For a tense moment it looked as though the Russians might use force to counteract this nationalist revolt of Poland's Communists. But as there were threats of large-scale popular unrest, Gomulka succeeded not only in getting the Soviet leaders to withdraw their forces to the frontiers, but also in calming down his compatriots. National elections were scheduled for 1957; political prisoners were pardoned; Soviet officers who held high posts in the Polish armed forces were removed; and Cardinal Wyszynski was freed after three years' detention. Here, then, was an example of how to achieve at least partial freedom from Soviet interference. It was this example of Poland that inspired the Hungarians to try for similar concessions.

The situation in Hungary was far more complicated. There, too, a great deal of resentment had built up, not only against Russian domination, but against communism in general. The peasants hated collectivization, the workers suffered from a low standard of living, and everyone opposed the antireligious policy of the Communist regime. Control of the Hungarian Communist movement had long been contested between Matyas Rakosi, a dedicated Stalinist, and Imre Nagy, a Communist with strong nationalist leanings. After Stalin's death Nagy had become premier of Hungary, but in 1955 Rakosi had taken over. In 1956 Rakosi, too, was forced to give way, but his replacement, Erno Gerö, while anti-Stalinist, was still a loyal follower of Moscow. When the news of Poland's successful rebellion reached Budapest in late October, therefore, thousands of Hungarians, especially students and workers, demanded the reinstatement of Nagy. The Gerö government immediately invited Soviet troops to help restore order. To satisfy the rioters, however, the Communist Central Committee also made Nagy premier. Nagy thereupon promised "democratization and improved living standards" and urged the crowds to disperse. But the rioters refused to go home. When they were fired upon by Soviet tanks, they fought back with arms supplied by the Hungarian army. From Budapest the rebellion spread to the provinces, and from an initial fight against the Russians, the revolt now turned against communism as such. Premier Nagy continued his efforts to restore calm. He invited two non-Communists into his government and promised free elections and the establishment of a multi-party system. Still more important, he succeeded in getting the Russians to withdraw their tanks from Budapest.

Up to this point the Hungarian revolt, in its general outlines, had followed the Polish example. Moscow, moreover, now announced sweeping concessions for all its subject peoples. The Soviet Union admitted that in its dealings with the satellites it had committed "violations and mistakes which belittled the principle of equality." Instead, Russia's leaders now proposed to regulate their economic relations with eastern Europe in such a way as to recognize "national sovereignty, mutual advantage, and equality." They declared their readiness to revise the Warsaw Pact so as to eliminate the further stationing of Soviet troops on satellite soil. The aim of the Soviet Union, this hopeful pronouncement concluded, was to create a "Commonwealth of Socialist States," bound together by ties of ideology and common interests rather than force.

But no sooner had this astounding confession of guilt and promise of reform been made, than the Russians again reversed their course. Hungarian insurgents had continued their fight against the withdrawing Soviet forces, and in their ransacking of Communist headquarters, the revolutionaries had made plain their anticommunism. It was this anti-Communist, as well as anti-Russian, nature of the Hungarian revolt that prompted Russia's renewed reprisals. On November 1 the Russians turned their tanks around and proceeded to put down the revolt. Premier Nagy thereupon repudiated the Warsaw Pact, declared Hungary a neutral country, and appealed to the United Nations to help defend Hungarian neutrality. But the Western powers at the time were preoccupied with events in the Middle East, where the Suez crisis was reaching its climax (see p. 164). On November 4 the Russians launched a full-scale offensive against Budapest, unleashing a reign of terror against the insurgents and against all Communists who had strayed from the pro-Moscow course. Some 35,000 persons were imprisoned, hundreds were put to death, and 186,000 of the freedom fighters fled abroad. A new Communist dictatorship was set up under Janos Kadar, and Imre Nagy and his associates were executed upon orders from Moscow.

THE SATELLITES UNDER KHRUSHCHEV

There have been no major outbreaks of resistance to communism in eastern Europe since 1956. Yet even though the satellite system withstood its gravest crisis and Russia continued to rule supreme, the liberalization that we have seen at work in Soviet domestic affairs continued also to be felt in the satellite countries. The basic Communist aim of economic development through heavy industry and collectivization remains the same today as under Stalin. But a good many concessions have been made in recent years to counteract the discontent that had culminated in the risings in Poland and Hungary. Terrorist methods and purges, so common under Stalin, have been abandoned; efforts are being made to improve living standards by raising wages, increasing social security benefits, and making available more consumer goods and better housing; and there has been much relaxation of cultural orthodoxy. The Soviet Union is counting on the nations of the Communist bloc to play their part in the drive to challenge the economic lead of the West. While under Stalin the satellites were exploited as tributaries, they have since become beneficiaries of some Soviet aid; and where in the past they were mere puppets of Moscow, they are now junior partners in a joint enterprise. The hold which the Soviet Union and communism have over the satellites differs in each country. The ones closest to Russia today are Poland, Hungary, and Bulgaria. Moscow's relations with East Germany and Czechoslovakia are also close, but not without occasional signs of friction. Romania in recent years has pulled away from the Communist bloc and drawn closer to the West. Albania, finally, has broken completely with Moscow and has joined Red China in its ideological quarrel with the Soviet Union.

For a while after 1956 it seemed as though Wladyslaw Gomulka might become another Tito and Poland another Yugoslavia. Just as in Yugoslavia, collectivization in Poland was abandoned, industrial management was decentralized, economic aid from the West was welcomed, and a measure of cultural freedom was granted. Since then, however, this trend has been abandoned. Under the Polish Seven-Year Plan (1959–65) the state again tightened its grip on the economy in an attempt to double or even triple production in certain key industries. Some efforts are again being made at collectivization; and "anti-Socialist influences" in the cultural sphere are being discouraged. Still Poland continues to occupy a unique position halfway between a satellite and a true ally of the Soviet Union. Most of her agriculture is still in private hands, and efforts to divert the Poles from their strong adherence to Catholicism have proved fruitless thus far. Poland has received substantial economic aid from the United States, for which the

Polish people have expressed their gratitude. Their government, on the other hand, has repaid American kindness with frequent anti-Western tirades. Gomulka and his Polish United Workers' (Communist) Party are trying to steer a careful course between keeping their people quiet and satisfying the Russians. The latter still have troops on Polish soil, and on all essential issues of foreign policy Poland follows the Soviet lead. It is with Soviet support alone that Poland can hope to resist future German claims for the return of the large territories that Poland took from Germany after World War II.

In Hungary the memory of the tragic events of 1956 lives on, even though the outward signs of the uprising have been carefully erased. Russia and some of the other Communist states have bolstered the government of Janos Kadar with massive economic aid, and the Hungarian people on the whole are living better today than they have for some years past. Industrialization has been fostered, and collectivization has made rapid progress since 1958. Kadar has invited popular support by declaring as his slogan: "Whoever is not against us is with us"; he has relaxed some of the more onerous restrictions of the past; and he has expelled many prominent Stalinists from the Hungarian Communist Party. Relations with the West have improved, especially since the United Nations in 1963 decided to end its opposition to the Kadar regime. However, Hungary, like Poland, is still firmly within the Russian orbit. Soviet armed forces are still present; half of Hungary's foreign trade is with the Soviet Union; and Kadar has stood loyally by the Russians in their dispute with the Chinese and Albanians.

The most docile of all the Soviet satellites is Bulgaria. Its friendship with Russia actually goes back before communism and into the nineteenth century. A poor and backward country, Bulgaria has made outwardly impressive progress under its Communist regime. Industry, which in 1939 accounted for only one-fourth of national production, now exceeds agricultural output almost three-fold. But much of this expansion has been artificial and poorly planned, based on Soviet aid, and at the expense of stagnation in an almost totally collectivized agriculture. Living standards are low, even by Communist standards, and some basic foods are still rationed. Bulgaria's leading Communist and premier, Todor Zhivkov, a mediocrity, has described the friendship between Bulgaria and Russia as "the sun and air of our people." Few Bulgarians would agree.

East Germany and Czechoslovakia are in a different category. As the leading industrial nations among the satellites, they are of greatest importance to the Soviet development scheme. The so-called German Democratic Republic, firmly controlled by Communist boss Walter Ulbricht, is in many ways the most completely sovietized of all the satellites. Emphasis on heavy industry and forced collectivization have caused periodic shortages of consumer goods and food, and repeated promises to catch up with the West German standard of living have remained unfulfilled. While falling short of its economic potential, East Germany nevertheless plays a key role in the economy of the Soviet bloc. She is Russia's main trading partner, and about 80 per cent of her exports go to Communist countries. The presence of twenty-two Soviet divisions, furthermore, makes East Germany the major base of Soviet military power in eastern Europe. The East Germans are deeply opposed to the Ulbricht regime, as evidenced by the close to six million refugees who fled to the West before 1961. Since then the Berlin wall has prevented large-scale defections, although individual escapes continue. The political and economic insecurity of his regime have made Ulbricht depend heavily on Russian support. In 1964 East Germany and Russia signed a treaty of friendship, cooperation, and mutual assistance, designed chiefly to bolster the unpopular Ulbricht regime. There have been occasional signs of disagreement between the two governments, especially over Russia's policy on Berlin, where Ulbricht wanted a firmer stand than Khrushchev was ready to take.

Czechoslovakia in the 1950's was the most prosperous of the satellites, and the government of Antonin Novotny, while hardly more popular than Communist regimes elsewhere, was tolerated for that reason. Since 1961, however, Czechoslovakia's economy has stagnated and in some phases has begun to decline, making life in that civilized country dull and drab. The reasons for this standstill are seen by Western observers in economic overextension and in passive resistance, or at least insufficient support, on the part of a freedom-loving people. What the Czechs and Slovaks object to in particular is the enforced eastward orientation of the country's economy under the direction of the Soviet-sponsored Council for Mutual Economic Assistance (COMECON) and the economic drain resulting from foreign aid to underdeveloped countries in Asia, Africa, and Latin America. To meet this criticism, the government in 1963 began to follow a more liberal course at home and to reduce foreign aid abroad. Czechs also were allowed to travel more freely. The resulting "thaw" was criticized by the Soviet Union for the "excessive freedom" it gave to intellectuals.

Objection to COMECON has also been behind much of Romania's alienation from the Soviet Union. The Council for Mutual Economic Assistance, as we have seen, was founded in 1949 as a counterpart to the American-sponsored European Recovery Program (see p. 24). As western Europe began to integrate its economies behind the Common Market, the Soviet bloc tried to keep pace by drawing together the various satellite economies and arranging for an "international socialist division of labor" among them. Under the direction of COMECON, East Germany and Czechoslovakia thus were to produce capital goods, machinery, and such, in return for raw materials from the Soviet Union and some of the other satellites. There was to be a common electric power network and a 2,500-mile "pipeline of friendship" to deliver Russian oil to eastern Europe. Most of the satellites did not dare to oppose a program which was obviously geared to Russia's advantage. The only country that refused to fall in line was Romania. Efficiently run by Communist leader Gheorghe Gheorghiu-Dej, Romania at home had followed a strictly "Stalinist" course of industrial planning combined with collectivization in agriculture. In its foreign trade policy, however, Romania had steadfastly defied the efforts of COMECON to integrate her economy with the rest of eastern Europe. Early in 1964 Romania went so far as to issue a virtual declaration of independence from Soviet influence. This was followed by an agreement with the United States for the purchase, on credit, of American industrial equipment. At the same time Romania also refused to align herself firmly with Moscow in the latter's fight with Peking, but instead preferred to maintain a neutral stand.

Romania's assertion of independence was not the only sign of change within the seemingly monolithic Communist bloc. A far more serious break had already occurred earlier between Russia and Albania. That small, poor, and backward country has always relied on some larger power for protection and assistance. After World War II the role of protector was first assumed by Yugoslavia. When the latter broke with Russia in 1948, however, Albania's Communists under Enver Hoxha sided with Stalin. For the next ten years Russia and some of the other satellites gave Albania the economic help she so desperately needed. Albania's main advantage to the Soviet Union was strategic, providing a Mediterranean base for Soviet submarines. With the advent of Khrushchev, Russo-Albanian relations deteriorated. As an ardent Stalinist, Hoxha resented Khrushchev's denunciation of the dead dictator and was suspicious of Russia's rapprochement with Yugoslavia. The actual severance of relations between the two countries developed slowly and was not completed until late in 1961. By that time Russia had withdrawn all aid from Albania, had severed diplomatic relations, and had caused Albania to be expelled from the Warsaw Pact and the Council of Mutual Economic Assistance. Meanwhile Albania had found a new protector in Communist China, who supplied the aid and technicians which Russia had withdrawn. Albania, in return, supported Red China in its verbal battles with Khrushchev.

The defection of Albania ended Russia's single hold over eastern Europe. There had, of course, been the break with Yugoslavia in 1948, but that, as we have seen, had been healed after Stalin's death. For a while it appeared as though the rapprochement was only temporary. In an attempt to assert his continued independence, Tito in 1958 issued a program for the Yugoslav Communist Party which denied the Soviet Union's claim to leadership in the Communist world, accused the Soviet state of violating some basic concepts of Marxist-Leninist theory, and blamed the East as much as the West for the international tension of the cold war. Moscow's reaction to this criticism was to turn its back once again on Tito. By 1961 Tito had clearly emerged as a neutralist, although he has denied that there is such a thing. "There can be no neutral nations," he has said. "That does not mean one must belong to a power bloc. . . . one can cooperate with everyone." That is exactly what Yugoslavia has been doing in recent years. She has dissociated herself from her military commitments to Greece and Turkey and has renounced military aid from the United States, while welcoming continued economic aid. Beginning in 1962 relations between Tito and Khrushchev returned to where they had been before 1958, with Tito once again a member in good standing of the Communist family, but an independent member, not a Russian satellite. The fact that Tito's "national communism" had been just as much a target of Red China's attacks as Khrushchev's "coexistence" did much to help bring about this renewed rapprochement.

It is difficult to make any final evaluation of the changes that have taken place in Russia's relations with her satellites during the Khrushchev era. One thing is certain: The firm grip which Stalin

had on eastern Europe has been loosened to the point where terms
like "Communist bloc" or even "satellites" have lost much of their
validity. There are various reasons for this change: the reassertion
of nationalism in eastern Europe; the example of first Yugoslavia
and then Albania successfully challenging Soviet leadership; the
economic difficulties that have beset some of the Communist regimes of eastern Europe, leading in some cases to renewed economic contacts with the West; and, finally, the ideological confusion created in the Communist camp by the split between the
Soviet Union and Communist China. The changes in eastern
Europe in the last decade may be summed up this way: While
under Stalin it was expected that every eastern European Communist regime imitate and follow the lead of the Soviet Union as
closely as possible, today such conformity is expected only in what
the Russians consider essential. The fact remains that the Eastern
countries, including Yugoslavia, are still Communist and as such are
worlds apart from the free Western world. Furthermore, except
for Yugoslavia and Albania, they all have close economic and military ties with the Soviet Union. As long as these ties remain intact,
the Russians apparently have no objection if additional connec-
tions are made with the capitalist world. Only if the approach to
the West should go too far and result in a cutting of the wires to
Moscow will the Russians feel their own interests sufficiently
threatened to step in and use force in order to insure continued
conformity. There is no sign that such action will be necessary in
the near future.

5

THE COMMONWEALTH LEADERS:
A FAMILY PORTRAIT

Taken at the annual conference of Commonwealth leaders
in 1964.* The Commonwealth, successor
to a mighty empire, continues to be an agency for
fruitful collaboration between white and colored peoples.

WIDE WORLD PHOTOS.

*On the first level, from l.: Milton Obote, Uganda; Sir Alec Douglas-Home,
Great Britain; Jomo Kenyatta, Kenya; Mrs. Bandaranaike, Ceylon. Second
level: Tunku Abdul Rahman (glasses), Malaysia; Sir Robert Menzies, Australia;
Eric Williams (dark glasses), Trinidad and Tobago; Dr. Hastings Banda, Malawi;
and Kwame Nkrumah (dark tunic), Ghana. Third level: Keith Holyoake, New
Zealand; T. T. Krishnamachari, India; Spyros Kyprianou, Cyprus; and D. B.
Sangster, Jamaica. Top level: Lester Pearson, Canada; Sir Abubakar Tafawa
Balewa, Nigeria; Field Marshal Mohammed Ayub Khan, Pakistan; and Julius
Nyerere (visible behind Khan), Tanzania.

THE END
OF COLONIALISM

THE MOST NUMEROUS AND IMPORTANT political changes since World War II have taken place in Asia and Africa. One after another, peoples that had never known political independence, or had lost such independence long ago, have won their freedom in the last twenty years. As a result, the number of the world's sovereign states has grown by more than fifty. Colonialism today is very much a thing of the past. There are many reasons for the success of these native revolts: the weakening of the Western colonial powers as a result of the war; the spread of communism as a rival force to Western capitalism; the rise of a Western-educated native intelligentsia providing the necessary leadership in the struggle for independence; and, most important, the growth of nationalism among the peoples of Asia and Africa. The actual events of the various native revolts have differed widely and will be treated separately. Yet almost all the new nations that have thus sprung into existence have been equally concerned with three major issues: (1) opposition to any form of colonialism, that is, rule of whites over nonwhites; (2) demand for full racial and political equality; and (3) need for economic and technical aid. In their relations with the rest of the world, on the other hand, these nations have followed quite different courses. Some of them have aligned themselves with one or the other side in the cold war. But the majority of them have preferred to maintain an independent, neutral position. This enables them to bargain for help from both East and West and to assume the role of a potential "third force" in the global balance of power.

INDIA AND PAKISTAN

The first major additions to the community of free nations after World War II came in 1947, when India, Britain's most valuable colony, changed into the two sovereign Dominions of India and Pakistan. India's struggle for independence dates back before World War I. It was led by the colony's largest political party, the Indian National Congress, under British-educated Mohandas K. Gandhi and Jawaharlal Nehru. The problem of independence was complicated by the extreme diversity of the vast subcontinent with its more than 400 million people, who speak at least thirty different languages. Aside from the regions directly administered by the British, there were more than five hundred native states under indirect British rule. In addition, the French and Portuguese held some small bases along the Indian coast. The population of India was divided by a rigid caste system, by wide extremes of wealth and poverty, and by religious differences between a Hindu majority and a large Moslem minority. The latter, organized in the Moslem League under Mohammed Ali Jinnah, feared suppression by the Hindus and thus wanted their own independent Moslem state of Pakistan.

The struggle for independence reached its culmination during World War II. Britain, recognizing the inevitable, was willing to set India free, but to prevent internal chaos insisted that a workable government be set up first. As a transition measure the British at the end of the war sponsored the election of a constituent assembly in which both Hindus and Moslems were represented. In early 1947 the British government announced its intention of transferring governmental power into Indian hands not later than the middle of 1948. Hindu-Moslem differences over the future of India, meanwhile, combined with serious food shortages, caused frequent riots and thousands of deaths. Gandhi himself was killed by a religious fanatic. By August 15, 1947, the process of partition was completed, and on that day both India and Pakistan were made into Dominions, that is, fully sovereign states. They were to remain members of the Commonwealth for one year, after which they were free to withdraw. India in 1949 became a federal republic, the Union of India, but decided to stay within the Commonwealth. Pakistan in 1956 followed India's example and likewise became a republic. The large number of native states were given the choice of setting up a third independent state or joining either India or Pakistan. They adopted the second alternative, most of them joining India.

The island of Ceylon off the southeast coast of India, in the past administered separately from British India, was granted self-government in 1946 and was admitted to full Dominion status in 1948. In its foreign policy the government of Ceylon at first leaned to the West. Since 1956, however, it has taken a neutralist stand and drawn closer to the Communist powers. This leftward trend continued after the victory of the socialist Sri Lanka Freedom Party under Mrs. Sirimavo Bandaranaike in 1960. Nationalization of United States oil company facilities in 1963 led to suspension of American economic aid to Ceylon. The country continued to receive assistance from several Communist nations as well as from the Commonwealth. There has been some thought of changing Ceylon from a Dominion into a republic, but not of taking her out of the Commonwealth.

As for the small French and Portuguese holdings on the Indian mainland, France relinquished her foothold in 1954, and India took possession of the Portuguese territory of Goa in 1961. One area that has caused much trouble between India and Pakistan as well as between these two and Communist China is the former native state of Kashmir in the extreme north. Its people are predominantly Moslem. When the Hindu Maharajah of Kashmir sought to join the region to India, Moslem tribesmen from Pakistan invaded Kashmir, where they became involved in war with Hindu forces from India. The United Nations intervened and in 1949 was able to negotiate a cease-fire. India and Pakistan agreed on a plebiscite to determine the status of Kashmir, but sporadic border clashes have continued, and the plebiscite has never been held.

India, meanwhile, is holding the richest two-thirds of Kashmir, while Pakistan controls the rest. When Communist China in 1959 laid claim to some territory along its own borders with Kashmir, India and Pakistan increased their efforts to settle their dispute. But even China's attack on India in 1962 did not bring India and Pakistan closer together. All attempts at mediation have failed thus far, as India continues to claim most of Kashmir, while Pakistan would like to see the region's future determined by plebiscite.

There have been other difficulties between India and Pakistan, caused chiefly by the hurried withdrawal of the British and the almost impossible task of dividing India's assets between the two new states. Differences over the waters of the Indus River, which both countries claimed for irrigation purposes, were settled by compromise in 1960. Additional problems arose over the exchange of nearly twelve million Moslems and Hindus, which led to a murderous civil war, especially in the Punjab region. The resulting tensions have made peaceful collaboration between India and Pakistan extremely difficult. Yet at the same time the two are closely interdependent. Pakistan holds much of the strategic northern frontier and most of the best agricultural lands, while India has the more valuable natural and industrial resources and the manpower to defend the subcontinent against further Communist encroachment from the north.

The Union of India, with an area one-third the size of the United States and a population of 460 million, is by far the more important of the two states. Because of Britain's long-standing practice of using Indians at all lower administrative levels, the change of regimes, except for the consequences of partition, went smoothly. Under the capable leadership of Prime Minister Nehru, democratic government took a firm hold. When Nehru died in 1964, the Congress Party chose Lal Bahadur Shastri to succeed him. Although able and respected, Shastri lacks his predecessor's magnetic appeal and large personal following. The Congress Party has been able to maintain a safe parliamentary majority. Opposition parties are too numerous and divided to wield much influence. Communism, considering the country's poverty, has not been a serious threat, although Communist influence in some states, such as Kerala, has been strong. India's main problems have been economic. Its large population, growing at the rate of almost ten million each year, and still mostly illiterate, is desperately poor and undernourished. Food shortages, hunger, and even starvation are constant threats. The government is doing its best through measures ranging from birth control to land reform and industrialization. But since India refrains scrupulously from limiting individual freedom, progress has been slow. An added difficulty has been the persistence of social customs and practices officially outlawed, such as the caste system and the subjection of women.

In its efforts to improve the country's economy, the Indian government has followed the Communist practice of state planning through five-year plans. Its major reforms have been concentrated on agriculture. Policies have varied between the very effective community projects (improving farming methods, largely with American aid) and the less effective movement of land distribution advocated by Shri Vinoba Bhave, a disciple of Gandhi. In industry the main emphasis has been on basic industries and long-range public projects. The effect of such projects will take time to be felt. India has abundant natural resources that have hardly begun to be developed. What she needs more than anything is foreign capital. The United States has contributed more than four billion dollars to India's economic development, and in recent years the Soviet Union, too, has supplied large funds. Even with such outside help, however, India still has a long, hard road ahead. If she succeeds in her efforts, she will have proved to the other underdeveloped countries that progress can be made through economic planning without paying the heavy price of communism.

In her foreign relations India has followed a course of non-alignment with either side in the cold war. The architect of this policy was Prime Minister Nehru. His basic aims were laid down in the famous "five principles" formulated in 1954: "Respect for other countries' territorial integrity and sovereignty; nonaggression; non-interference in other nations' internal affairs; equality and mutual benefit; and peaceful coexistence." Despite this declaration of neutrality, India has at times seemed to lean more toward the East than toward the West. To understand India's position, we must remember her traditional policy of nonviolence, inherited from the days of Gandhi; her long and hard firsthand experience with Western colonialism; and the fact that India is situated much closer to China and Russia than to the West. Still, in recent years Indians have come to take a somewhat less favorable view of communism. The first disillusionment came with Russia's ruthless intervention in Hungary. This was followed by China's similar action in Tibet. Finally, India herself became the victim of Communist aggression when, beginning in 1959, Red China started to advance into some border regions in Kashmir and in the area of India's Northeast Frontier Agency. Attempts to settle these differences by negotiation have failed, and at present an uneasy cease-fire exists along the India-China frontier. Nevertheless, India's relations with Red China remain outwardly correct, and she continues to profess friendship for the Soviet Union.

While India tried to steer a middle course in world affairs, Pakistan, in the beginning at least, seemed firmly committed to the West. During the first decade of her independence, Pakistan went through troubled times. With the death of Mohammed Ali Jinnah in 1948 the country lost its most capable political leader. Representative government existed in name only, as professional politicians ruled an illiterate population to suit their own ambitions. In 1958 the army finally stepped in, dissolved Parliament, and proclaimed martial law. Since then Pakistan has been under the authoritarian rule of British-trained General Mohammed Ayub Khan. A new constitution in 1962 called for a National Assembly; but it was elected by only a small percentage of the people and its powers are limited. Elections on the basis of a more general franchise have been promised for 1965.

Pakistan's political instability has slowed down her economic development. The country, only one-third the size of India, is divided into two areas separated by a thousand miles of Indian territory. The two parts have little in common, except their Moslem religion. East Pakistan, although only one-sixth as large as West Pakistan, contains 55 per cent of the country's total population of close to ninety-five million. This inequality has been the source of much discontent. About 80 per cent of Pakistanis are farmers, most of them illiterate and very poor. Pakistan has few natural resources, and industrialization is still in its beginnings. Yet the rate of growth in recent years, thanks to foreign aid, has been high and, in contrast to India, has exceeded the rate of population growth. A third Five-Year Plan, covering the years 1965–70, calls for an outlay of close to nine billion dollars.

Pakistan has been a member, from the outset, of both the Southeast Asia and the Central Treaty organizations. In the last few years, however, there has been a noticeable shift away from a pro-Western toward a pro-Communist or at least pro-neutralist position. Resentment of Western aid to India, Pakistan's chief rival, has been the main reason for this realignment. Beginning in 1962

Pakistan concluded a number of agreements with Red China, the most important of which settled the border dispute between the two countries over Kashmir. She has also signed economic agreements with the Soviet Union and with some of the Communist countries of eastern Europe. At the same time Pakistan still depends heavily on American aid, and for that if no other reason continues to be an ally of the West, albeit a disgruntled one.

COMMUNIST CHINA

Of still greater importance than the emancipation of India from three centuries of British rule has been the emergence of Communist China as a major factor in international affairs. We have already discussed the Chinese Civil War and the establishment of the People's Republic of China in 1949 (see Chapter 1). Despite Red China's exhaustion from fighting against both Chiang Kai-shek and Japan, the new regime almost immediately became involved in another conflict in Korea. The Korean war cost China an estimated 840,000 casualties and 2.4 billion dollars and put China under a partial economic embargo at a most critical time. Despite these initial difficulties the Communists were able to complete their subjugation of some six hundred million Chinese, an achievement that testifies to the inherent strength of Chinese communism.

The communization of China was a gradual process, involving not only a complete political and economic change, but also a social and psychological transformation. The first years of the new regime, aside from economic reconstruction and the Korean war, were devoted mainly to "purifying" the ranks of China's Communists, reducing the power of the middle class, and "remolding" the minds of Chinese intellectuals along Marxist lines. Such age-old Chinese vices as "corruption, waste, and bureaucratism" were attacked, and bribery, tax evasion, and stealing of state property were eradicated. Combining terror with persuasion, this policy of "criticism and self-criticism" succeeded in converting the majority of Chinese into obedient followers, and in many cases, supporters, of the new regime.

In organizing their government, China's Communists closely followed the Russian model. Under the constitution of 1954 "supreme state power" is vested in a "National People's Congress" of 1,200 elected members. The influence of this body, however, is as insignificant as that of Russia's Supreme Soviet. Executive power is in the hands of the chairman of the republic (president)—a post held until 1959 by Mao Tse-tung and since then by Liu Shao-chi—and of a State Council (cabinet) under Premier Chou En-lai. As in Russia, the real power rests with the Communist Party. Its membership in 1965 was over seventeen million. The party is dominated by its Central Committee and its chairman, Mao Tse-tung. This peasant's son—at once poet and politician, classical scholar and warlord, Marxist theoretician and ruthless dictator—is thus the most powerful man in Communist China. Next to Mao there are a handful of other key figures. Besides Liu Shao-chi and Chou En-lai, these include Chu Teh, for years leader of the Chinese Red Army, Chen Yun, the party's chief spokesman on economic policy, Teng Hsiao-ping, secretary general of the party, and Lin Piao, minister of defense. These men, together with Mao Tse-tung, form the standing committee of the party's eighteen-man Politburo and exercise a kind of collective leadership.

According to the constitution, the main task of the Chinese state is "to bring about, step by step, the socialist industrialization of the country." This goal was to be achieved in three five-year plans. The first of these, covering the years 1953 through 1957, went under the slogan "production and austerity," which well describes all of Communist China's economic policy. China's economy in the past had been predominantly agrarian. To win the support of the peasants, one of the first acts of the Communists had been to divide the large holdings of the former landlords. Since this interfered with efficient production, however, the first Five-Year Plan called for a change from individual cultivation toward large-scale collectivization. By the end of 1957 agricultural output still lagged, but industry had made considerable strides, increasing its yearly production by an estimated 25 per cent. In some industries, notably steel, the rate of growth had been such that Communist China predicted she would soon catch up with other important industrial powers such as Britain and Japan.

At this point, in 1958, the Chinese government embarked on its second Five-Year Plan, advertised as "the great leap forward." Its primary attention was directed at agriculture, to help feed the nation's huge population, by now exceeding 700 million and growing at the rate of 16 million each year. The most novel feature of the great leap was the formation of the so-called people's communes. These were large mergers of collective farms, including

146

several thousand peasant households and covering many square miles. The purpose of these new social units was first and foremost to make for greater efficiency and output in agriculture. The ultimate aim of the communes, however, was more than economic. Through strict regimentation and collective living, China's traditional family system was to be eradicated. Members of a commune were to work and live together; their children were to be raised in communal nurseries; work was supplemented by drill in a communal militia; and with all basic needs supplied, wages could be cut to a minimum. Here was a wholly new form of Communist society, more revolutionary than anything ever seen in Russia. The commune system is the ultimate in Communist control. The individual becomes a mere cog in a monstrous machine, geared toward greater and greater production. His fate is to work and obey, to live and endure.

The great leap, which started on a wave of semi-hysteria in 1958, soon turned into a big slump. There were some initial achievements in industry, but these were counteracted by disastrous failures in agriculture. Some of these were due to natural calamities, floods and droughts; but the main reasons for the breakdown were faulty planning, shortage of essential machinery and fertilizer, and, most important, a too rapid shift from collectives to communes. Communist China by the end of its great leap in 1960 was back where she had started three years earlier, except that in the interim her population had grown by another thirty to forty million. To recover from this major setback, China's rulers since then have been concentrating on such phases of industrial development—electrification, production of farm, irrigation, and drainage machinery, and fertilizers—as are prerequisite to any lasting agricultural improvement. Such a shift, however, has been at the expense of over-all industrial growth. At the same time the commune system has been radically changed. Production is again carried on in smaller brigades and teams of peasants; communal living has been de-emphasized; and peasant families have been given back some land and a few domestic animals for their own use. It remains to be seen to what extent this relaxation of pressure is merely a temporary effort to improve peasant morale or a lasting change in policy.

There can be no doubt that the Communist regime is strong enough to enforce any measure it feels necessary, no matter how harsh. Mao Tse-tung has admitted that his government has liquidated more than 800,000 persons. Western sources put the number of victims at between ten and twenty million. A population ruled by terror, however, can hardly be expected to achieve the optimistic goals which its Communist rulers have set for themselves. The Communists, therefore, have perfected more subtle ways of "socialist re-education" through indoctrination and brainwashing. In 1957 Mao Tse-tung startled the world by conceding that not all was harmonious even in a Communist society. There may be "contradictions," he said, "between the masses of the people and their leaders." To resolve these contradictions they must be brought into the open. "Let a hundred flowers bloom," the Chinese leader said, "let a hundred schools of thought contend." The people must be encouraged to speak their minds so that their grievances may be known and corrected. This invitation to let off steam actually brought some outspoken criticism of the regime; but when this criticism became too violent, Mao turned against the crops of "poisonous weeds" that crowded out the flowers, and the campaign of self-criticism was abandoned.

One of the most effective means of quieting discontent at home is to turn it against real or imaginary enemies abroad. The main target of Red China's attacks from the very start has been the United States. American-Chinese tension has several causes in addition to the fact that Americans and Chinese have fought each other in Korea. The United States has steadfastly refused to recognize Red China and continues to support the Nationalist Chinese regime of Chiang Kai-shek on Taiwan; she has stood firm against admission of Communist China to the United Nations; and she has imposed an embargo on trade with the Chinese mainland. The Communists, on their side, have made the usual charges of American "imperialism," have accused the United States of using germ warfare in Korea, and have arrested a number of Americans as alleged spies. There have been several occasions since Korea when the United States and China seemed on the verge of war. The main trouble at first was over the offshore islands between Taiwan and the mainland, especially Quemoy and Matsu. Since 1954 the Communists have intermittently bombarded these Nationalist outposts, and in 1958–59 a Communist invasion of the islands seemed imminent. The presence of the United States Seventh Fleet discouraged such action, however. Since then Red China has shifted its attention elsewhere, notably to Laos and Vietnam. Unceasing propaganda attacks upon the United States, meanwhile, help keep alive that air of tension which the Reds need in order to justify the many sacrifices they are demanding of their people.

While the United States was public enemy number one, the Soviet Union, in the beginning at least, was Communist China's greatest friend and benefactor. Under a thirty-year treaty of friendship signed in 1950, Russia helped China to build up a huge modern army and to carry out her sweeping program of industrialization. More than half of China's exports went to the U.S.S.R., and in return she received capital goods, technical aid, and military supplies. This honeymoon lasted until some time in the late 1950's, when a gradual cooling set in. As China began realizing some of her potentialities as a great power, she became less willing to accept Soviet leadership. The main differences between Peking and Moscow developed over the issue of peaceful coexistence. It had actually been Communist China that had developed the concept of coexistence in the early 1950's. But beginning in 1957, the Chinese started advocating a new, "hard" line, insisting that ultimate Communist victory could not be won through peaceful competition with capitalism, as Russia was now advocating, but only through militancy and, if need be, war. The Sino-Soviet dispute was basically one of ideology, with each side accusing the other of falsifying the true meaning of Marxism-Leninism. Yet there were also a number of specific issues. China complained about insufficient Russian aid, especially as the Soviets in 1960 began withdrawing their technical advisers while at the same time curtailing their trade with Communist China. In 1961 the Chinese protested Russia's denunciation of Albania at the Twenty-second Soviet Party Congress. In 1962 China accused the Soviet Union of siding with India in the Chinese-Indian border conflict. In 1963 there were even signs of possible border conflicts between Russia and China. The Chinese also claimed that Russia had gone back on an earlier promise to supply them with nuclear weapons. Instead China now stepped up research for an independent nuclear force, and in 1964 she exploded her first small atomic bomb.

Many of the issues just mentioned as having contributed to the widening rift between the Soviet Union and Communist China grew out of China's fundamental aim in foreign policy—to re-establish her ancient predominance in Asia. In her relations with the smaller Asian countries, Red China has tried to capitalize on the widespread opposition to colonialism by harping on a policy of "Asia for the Asians." Her simultaneous claims for border regions in India, Burma, and Nepal, however, have shown that China's primary aim is to extend her own sphere of power. The true nature of Chinese Communist rule became obvious in Tibet in 1959.

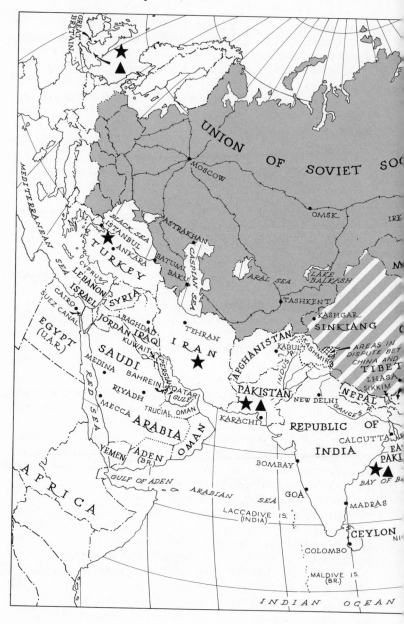

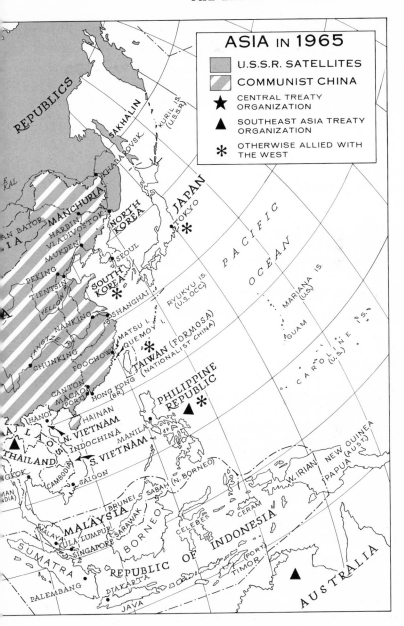

When the Chinese proceeded to communize Tibet's Buddhist society, sporadic violence flared into general rebellion. But the uprising was suppressed with utmost savagery, showing that the Chinese are every bit as ruthless in their aims and methods as the Russians. In recent years the Red Chinese have trodden more softly, using trade and aid to gain friends and influence. The mounting pressure of China's vast population demands an outlet. The most inviting region for Chinese expansion is the critical area of Southeast Asia.

NATIONALISM IN SOUTHEAST ASIA

Southeast Asia, the area east of India and south of China, is a wealthy region, inhabited by more than two hundred million people. It produces five-sixths of the world's natural rubber, more than half of its tin, two-thirds of its coconut products, and, most important, 60 per cent of the world's exportable rice. A look at the map shows Southeast Asia's important strategic location across the main lines of communication between Europe and the Far East. Most of the nations of Southeast Asia are new. Before 1945 only Thailand was independent. Since then the Philippines, Burma, Indonesia, Vietnam, Laos, Cambodia, and Malaysia have gained sovereignty. With the exception of Thailand, there have been Communist revolts in all of these countries. In the case of North Vietnam, Communist conquest has been successful.

Like all underdeveloped regions, Southeast Asia is predominantly agricultural. Except for Indonesia it does not as yet suffer from overpopulation. Its standard of living, while higher than in other parts of Asia, is still very low, and health conditions are extremely poor. What Southeast Asia needs most is to develop better-balanced national economies, with greater diversification (away from the limited number of staple commodities like rice, tin, or rubber) and increased industrialization. But such improvements are impeded by the general backwardness of the area, its racial and linguistic diversity, and its political instability. Nationalism has been a major force in Southeast Asia for several decades. But its victory, by removing the strong hand of the former colonial powers, has had a disruptive effect and has increased the danger of Communist expansion. At the same time opposition to colonialism makes some of the new nations of Southeast Asia reluctant to align themselves with their former masters. Instead, these countries prefer a policy of nonalignment, which further tends to weaken their power to resist communism.

In looking at the individual nations of Southeast Asia, we find a wide variety of political and economic problems that defy any further generalization. Some, like Thailand and the Philippines, have followed a relatively stable course. Thailand, never subject to colonial rule, is a constitutional monarchy with a king who is revered but has little power. In the last thirty years the country has seen a succession of more or less corrupt military regimes. The latest of these, headed by Field Marshal Sarit Thanarat, took over in 1958. Sarit differed from his predecessors in his sincere efforts to clean up the government. His work was continued after his death in 1963 by his deputy, General Thanom Kittikachorn. Thailand is a fertile and underpopulated land. The vast majority of its twenty-six million people are farmers, and most of them grow rice, which is Thailand's chief commodity of export. As a member of the Southeast Asia Treaty Organization, Thailand belongs to the Western camp. She has had trouble with her Chinese minority, some 15 per cent of the population, but compared to the rest of Southeast Asia, the politically passive Siamese lead contented lives.

The same does not quite hold true for the close to twenty-eight million Filipinos. The Philippine Republic was born on July 4, 1946, when the United States lived up to a promise made twelve years earlier of setting free its former possession. The government of the Philippines is closely modeled after that of the former mother country. There have been Communist disturbances, but since 1954 these have subsided. The most pressing problems of the young republic are economic. Due chiefly to the damage in World War II and the separation from the United States, Philippine recovery has been slow, and widespread poverty still prevails. Because of their potential wealth, greater degree of modernization, and sound democratic system, however, the Philippines are better off than most other Southeast Asian countries. In its foreign policy the Philippine Republic follows closely the lead of the United States with whom she signed a mutual defense pact in 1951. America has provided substantial economic and military aid.

The only country in Southeast Asia where a former colonial power succeeded in restoring its control after World War II was Malaya. There was no objection when British rule was resumed in 1945. But the war, in Malaya as everywhere else, had aroused a desire for autonomy. This the British granted in 1946 with the establishment of the Federation of Malaya. The country gained complete independence in 1957, when Malaya became a sovereign member of the Commonwealth. Six years later, in 1963, the Federation was enlarged by the British possessions in Singapore and on the island of Borneo and was renamed Malaysia. This enlargement was criticized at the time by the Philippines, who had some prior claims to parts of Borneo, and has been violently opposed since by Indonesia. Relations between Malaysia and Indonesia have remained tense, but continued presence of British troops in Borneo has discouraged any major Indonesian aggression. Malaysia relies chiefly on exports of rubber and tin to support its fast-growing population of some ten million. The government of Premier Abdul Rahman has embarked on a program of diversification and industrialization to make its economy more flexible.

While Thailand, the Philippines, and Malaysia have openly aligned themselves with the West, the rest of the Southeast Asian nations, with the exception of Communist North Vietnam and pro-Western South Vietnam, are officially neutral. Burma's break away from the British Empire in 1948 came as the result of amicable negotiations; and while she refused to join the Commonwealth, her relations with Great Britain remained cordial. The Union of Burma was founded as a federal republic with a parliamentary government. During the first fourteen years after independence Burma, except for two brief intervals, was led by Prime Minister U Nu, one of the outstanding leaders of postwar Asian nationalism. Like Thailand, Burma is underpopulated and one of the world's leading producers of rice. The standard of living of the twenty-three million Burmese is low, and the government has few funds for economic development. Burma also has serious political problems. The national unity that helped the Burmese gain independence in 1948 went to pieces shortly afterwards. After a decade of domestic strife and vain efforts to deal with communism, U Nu resigned his premiership in 1958, and General Ne Win formed an emergency government. After a number of urgent reforms, and after free and democratic elections in 1960, the general returned his power to U Nu. But the prime minister was unable to cope with the many divisive issues that plagued his country—rivalry among his followers, religious and ethnic disunity, and continued underground activity of Communist rebels. In 1962 the military, under Ne Win, resumed control, suspended the constitution, and established a dictatorship. To appeal to the masses, the new regime promised to make Burma into a "socialist society of affluence." Burma's foreign policy, while remaining officially neutral, is tending more and more toward the Communist camp, and some Western observers fear that the country may end up as a Communist satellite.

The biggest Southeast Asian nation is Indonesia, with some 18,000 islands and more than 100 million people. It is also the most disorganized. The Republic of Indonesia proclaimed its independence in 1945, after more than three centuries of Dutch rule. The Dutch did not easily let go of their prized possession. It took four years and a costly war before they recognized Indonesia's freedom. Even then relations between the Netherlands and Indonesia remained tense. In 1957 Indonesia seized more than a billion dollars worth of Dutch assets, and in 1960 she severed diplomatic relations with The Hague. The main cause for tension was Dutch refusal to yield Netherlands New Guinea, or West Irian, to Indonesia. The issue was finally settled in 1963 when United States and United Nations mediators awarded West Irian to Indonesia on the condition that its future be determined by plebiscite. The plebiscite has not yet been held.

As in so many former colonial countries, political inexperience and general backwardness have kept democracy from taking hold in Indonesia. The island nation has been ruled more or less dictatorially by President Achmed Sukarno, another of Asia's leading nationalists. Opposition parties have been banned, and parliament has been replaced by a Provisional People's Congress in which Nationalists, Moslem, and Communist forces are represented. Indonesia's well-organized Communist Party claims a membership of two million. President Sukarno, who had himself elected for life in 1963, has defined his ideology as belief in God, democracy, nationalism, social justice, and humanitarianism. There have been several revolts against his policy of "guided democracy," the most serious in Sumatra and Celebes in 1958.

Indonesia's political instability has increased her economic difficulties. Her output of sugar, rubber, tin, and rice has actually declined in recent years, and only petroleum production has gained. With more than half of her population living on Java, industrial development of the island is imperative. To make any headway, substantial foreign capital is needed. Private investment has been scared away by the socialist tendencies of the Sukarno regime and by a stifling system of economic control. Indonesia has used her neutralist position to attract government aid from both East and West. As Sukarno leaned more and more toward the Communists and became more and more critical of the United States, American aid was reduced and finally, in 1964, cut off. The country's indebtedness already is such that more than half of its gross national product is needed to repay foreign credits. Military preparations, first against the Dutch and more recently against Malaysia, have further strained an already unbalanced economy.

The most restless and unstable region of Southeast Asia has not been Indonesia but Indochina. A former French possession, intensively colonized during the past century, Indochina includes three nations: Vietnam, Laos, and Cambodia. Resistance to French rule after World War II was led by the League for the Independence of Vietnam. The Vietminh, as the League was called, consisted of many factions, but its most effective components were the Communists. In 1945 the Communist Vietminh leader, Ho Chi-minh, proclaimed a provisional Republic of Vietnam. French refusal to recognize the new regime was the signal for war. While French forces had little difficulty in restoring control over Laos and Cambodia, Vietnam became the scene of a drawn-out conflict. The French did most of the fighting, and the United States bore most of the cost. By 1954 most of northern Vietnam was in the hands of the Vietminh, and the same year the French suffered a major defeat at Dien Bien Phu. At this point an armistice was concluded, and under an accord reached at Geneva in 1954 Vietnam, Laos, and Cambodia were recognized as independent states. Vietnam was left divided into a Communist north and an anti-Communist south, eventually to be unified in free elections.

For a while it appeared as though the situation in Indochina had been stabilized. The government of President Ngo Dinh Diem in South Vietnam enjoyed popular support and with American aid embarked on a program of economic reform. But the Diem government lost its backing as it gradually developed into an oppressive family oligarchy. It was overthrown by a military coup in 1963. Meanwhile the Communist regime of North Vietnam under Ho Chi-minh had started an intensive guerilla campaign against Diem, using South Vietnamese Communists (the Vietcong) supported by North Vietnamese men and supplies. To halt this Communist threat, the United States poured money, supplies, and men into

South Vietnam. By 1964 American military "advisers" in Vietnam numbered sixteen thousand. To all intents and purposes the United States was at war with North Vietnam.

The threat of advancing Communism in Indochina was not limited to Vietnam. In Laos, most backward of all the Southeast Asian nations, an uneasy balance prevailed among armed factions of Communists (the Pathet Lao), rightists, and neutralists. To preserve peace, a fourteen-nation agreement signed at Geneva in 1962 called for a neutral coalition government of the three factions. But by 1964 this coalition had broken down, and the Pathet Lao, supported by North Vietnam, had resumed their offensive against the government. In Cambodia, finally, the situation was somewhat more peaceful but hardly more promising for the West. Its government, while supposedly neutral, followed an increasingly anti-Western course and in 1963 severed all but diplomatic relations with the United States.

The ultimate source of all these Communist advances in Southeast Asia was Communist China. A Communist victory in Indochina would open the door to possible Chinese expansion into Burma, Thailand, Malaysia, and Indonesia. The only way to prevent such expansion was through continued massive aid from the West plus cooperation among the nations threatened by communism. Yet racial, religious, and political differences made such cooperation difficult. A start was made as far back as 1950 with the Colombo Plan for Cooperative Economic Development in South and Southeast Asia. Its members, besides the Asian nations directly concerned, include the United States, Canada, Britain, Australia, New Zealand, and Japan. The plan, thus far, has provided more technical assistance than economic aid. In 1961 Malaya, the Philippines, and Thailand formed the Association of Southeast Asia (ASA) to further economic and cultural exchanges and to create a free trade area. But disagreement between Malaysia and the Philippines over Borneo soon affected its usefulness. The same held true for "Maphilindo," a grouping of Malaysia, the Philippines, and Indonesia first discussed in 1963, but again checked by nationalist rivalries, this time between Indonesia and Malaysia.

In the military field, too, efforts have been made to protect free Asia from communism. In 1954 the United States, Great Britain, France, Australia, New Zealand, Pakistan, Thailand, and the Philippines formed the Southeast Asia Treaty Organization (SEATO). Its parties agreed to coordinate their efforts for mutual defense against aggression and subversion. SEATO, however, does not obligate members to take military action, nor does it have permanently allocated forces or a supreme commander. Some of the most important non-Communist countries of Asia, moreover, are not members. SEATO, therefore, is not comparable in strength or significance to NATO, its European counterpart. To make sure that SEATO was not misconstrued as an attempt to suppress colonial nationalism, its members signed a separate declaration, the "Pacific Charter," which promised "to promote the self-government and to secure the independence of all countries whose people desire it and are able to undertake its responsibilities." Still more important was the assurance of the Charter that its signatories would help "to promote higher living standards, economic progress and social well-being" for Southeast Asia. Here lies the real answer to Southeast Asia's manifold troubles.

JAPAN AND KOREA

To round out our discussion of recent developments in the Far East, we must look briefly at two countries that have been particularly closely associated with American interests. We have already discussed the early postwar history of Japan (see pp. 29 ff.). Despite some domestic crises, mostly over foreign policy issues, the country's new democratic system has become firmly rooted, and its economy has made amazing strides. Direction of national affairs since 1948 has been in the hands of various conservative factions which, since 1955, have been united behind the Liberal-Democratic Party. Among the party's outstanding figures have been Nobusuke Kishi, prime minister from 1957 to 1960, and his successor, Hayato Ikeda. The main opposition comes from the Socialist Party, which has polled about 30 per cent of the popular vote in most elections. The Liberal-Democrats stand for free enterprise, the strengthening of national defense, and cooperation with the free world. The Socialists, on the other hand, would like to see gradual socialization, no rearmament, and a neutralist foreign policy. The Communist Party plays a negligible role in Japanese politics.

Japan's most remarkable achievements have been in the economic sphere. By the early 1960's, her national output since the end of the Allied occupation in 1952 had more than doubled, manufacturing had increased fourfold, food was abundant, and foreign trade was breaking all records. These developments put Japan in a unique category, much closer to the advanced industrialized countries of western Europe than to the underdeveloped nations of the Far East. The people of Japan, on the whole, have shared in the country's new prosperity, as living standards have risen steadily. Only housing continues to be a serious problem. Thanks to birth control and full employment, overpopulation is no longer a threat. Current plans of the Japanese government are for a doubling of per capita income by 1970. In the light of past developments there seems little doubt that this aim will be achieved.

In her foreign policy Japan continues to remain closely aligned with the United States. Under the Security Treaty of 1960 (originally signed in 1951) the United States is pledged to defend Japan, and Japan in return gives America the necessary facilities to do so. In 1965 some forty-five thousand American troops were still stationed in Japan. Public opinion at times has favored a more independent policy, and there were violent protests against the renewal of the Security Treaty in 1960. But since about 30 per cent of Japan's foreign trade is with the United States, the political and military alignment of the two countries has a sound economic basis which helps assure its continuation.

Compared to those in Japan, events in South Korea since the end of the Korean war have been far from peaceful. War damage was speedily repaired, thanks to American aid; but economic reconstruction soon lagged. The government of Syngman Rhee, first president of the Republic of Korea, proved inefficient, wasteful, and increasingly oppressive. In 1960 popular discontent and disapproval by the United States forced Rhee to resign. The Second Korean Republic was officially launched in August, 1960, with John M. Chang as premier of Korea's first truly parliamentary government. But Chang, too, was unable to cope with the country's deteriorating economic situation. In May, 1961, he was replaced by a military junta, ultimately headed by General Chung Hee Park. After two years of turmoil and a constitutional reform that strengthened the presidency, General Park was elected president of the Third Korean Republic in 1963. At the same time his Democratic Republican Party won a slim parliamentary majority. The new government's efforts to improve the Korean economy were not very successful, as prices continued to rise and gains in industry were offset by losses in agriculture. In foreign affairs South

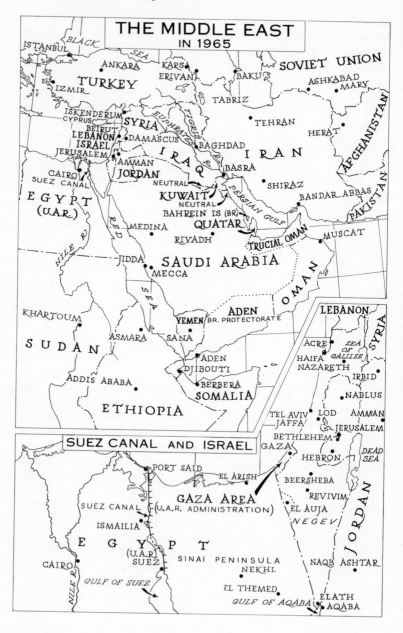

THE MIDDLE EAST
IN 1965

SUEZ CANAL AND ISRAEL

Korea remains closely tied to the United States. Her sizeable army, trained and equipped along United States lines, forms part of the United Nations forces in Korea. Tension along the truce line between North and South Korea continues, and the United States in 1965 still had more than twenty-six thousand men in Korea.

North Korea, by all accounts, is in far better shape economically than South Korea. The northern part has less than half the population of South Korea; it is not only larger, but has most of the country's industry and natural resources. The government of Kim Il-sung has received aid from both the Soviet Union and Communist China. In the doctrinal controversy between these two leading Communist powers North Korea has sided with Peking rather than with Moscow.

NATIONALISM IN THE MIDDLE EAST

One of the most turbulent scenes of rebellion against Western influence since World War II has been the Arab world and the Middle East, the area bridging the continents of Africa and Asia, from Morocco in the west to Iran in the east. It consists of three political sections: the Arab states, the non-Arab Moslem states, and Israel. We are here primarily concerned with the Arab states. Israel is really a Western community surrounded by a hostile and backward region. The young nation, through hard work and large amounts of foreign aid, has made tremendous strides in the first seventeen years of its independence. The non-Arab Moslem states —Turkey and Iran—are both old nations. Turkey underwent a thoroughgoing social and political revolution after World War I under the benevolent dictatorship of Mustafa Kemal Ataturk, who died in 1938. The first free elections in 1950 brought to power Premier Adnan Menderes, leader of the conservative Democratic Party. His increasingly repressive policy threatened to undo many of the gains which democracy had made in Turkey. In 1960, therefore, Menderes was ousted by an army junta, headed by General Cemal Gursel. A new constitution was proclaimed in 1961, and after free and democratic elections the Second Turkish Republic was launched with General Gursel as president and Ismet Inonu, one of Kemal Ataturk's oldest followers, as premier. Turkey continues to suffer from grave economic problems. Necessary changes have been impeded by a large and backward peasant population, deeply conservative and opposed to tax reforms, industrialization, and further Westernization. Because of her strategic situation astride the intercontinental waterway of the Bosporus and the Dardanelles, Turkey plays a key role in several Western defense organizations. Her position in NATO has been weakened because of the Turkish-Greek conflict over Cyprus and because of growing neutralist sentiment among younger Turks.

Iran, like Turkey, has been friendly to the West, though her relations with the Soviet Union also have improved in recent years. There were some signs of anticolonialism in Iran after World War II, especially during the premiership of Mohammed Mossadegh in 1952–53, when the Iranian parliament nationalized Britain's oil industry along the Persian Gulf. The matter was settled by a compromise in 1954. The leading political figure of Iran is Shah Mohammed Riza Pahlevi. Although he is a constitutional monarch, his influence is all but absolute. In an effort to combat Soviet propaganda the "reform shah" has done much to improve his country's economy. A six-point reform program in 1963 called for land reform, village education, nationalization and profit-sharing in some industries, and liberalization of the franchise. Opposition to this "white revolution" from some of the vested interests affected by these reforms has led to violent riots. The reforms have also tended to discourage foreign investment, and Iran continues to depend on aid from the United States. Communism, except during the time of Mossadegh, has not been a serious threat. Still, the poverty of the masses provides a fertile breeding ground for unrest and possibly revolution.

The Arab world of the Middle East is a harsh terrain of desert wilderness, broken by occasional fertile valleys and oases. It is inhabited by more than ninety million Arab Moslems, most of them desperately poor tenant farmers. Despite its economic backwardness, however, the Arab Middle East is of greatest importance. It lies across the shortest route between Europe and Asia; it contains about 50 per cent of the world's known oil resources; and it serves as the religious focus of more than three hundred million non-Arab Moslems living as far away as Southeast Asia. Outwardly the Arab world presents a certain unity, based on community of language, culture, and religion. But below the surface there are many divisive forces, chiefly due to rivalries among Arab leaders. The one sentiment that more than anything unites the Arab masses is their nationalism. And the strongest ingredient in this nationalism is hatred of any kind of foreign domination.

Before World War II only four of the Arab nations were independent, at least nominally: Egypt, Iraq, Saudi Arabia, and Yemen. Since then all the rest have won their freedom. Liberation from foreign control, however, did not solve the many problems of these countries. Arab society is still sharply divided into a tiny minority of extremely wealthy merchants and landowners and a huge mass of destitute peasants. Between these two extremes is a small, progressive middle class, mostly professional people educated in the West. Most of the Arab countries have excellent liberal constitutions, but these cannot conceal the basically authoritarian nature of their governments. Only after the dismally low standard of living of the Arab peoples has been raised can there be any hope for political changes in the direction of greater democracy. Economic development, however, can be achieved only with the aid of those very same foreigners whom Arab nationalism has been so eager to oust. To find a modus vivendi between Arabs and outsiders in the Middle East has been one of the concerns of international politics since World War II.

There is one issue on which the whole Arab world has seen eye to eye, and that is opposition to Israel. The outward manifestation of Arab unity has been the Arab League. Organized in 1945, it includes all thirteen of the Arab states. We have already discussed the Arab-Israeli war in 1948–49 (see Chapter 1). Subsequent border clashes led to a resumption of war between Israel and Egypt in 1956. Fighting was stopped once more by UN intervention, but intermittent border frictions have continued. Arab refugees in countries adjacent to Israel likewise present a major obstacle to any improved relations between the Arabs and Israel. United Nations attempts to integrate the more than one million refugees into their new surroundings have been resisted both by the refugees and by their fellow Arabs. A new issue arose in 1964 over Israel's plans to divert water from the Jordan River to irrigate the Negev Desert. Both Syria and Jordan claim the same water and have threatened reprisals by cutting off the Jordan's sources and starting their own reclamation projects.

While the Arabs present a common front against Israel, they are far from united on other issues. Most of the disputes within the Arab world have centered on its most powerful nation, Egypt. That country underwent a major change in 1952, when the Egyptian army overthrew the corrupt regime of King Farouk. The main force behind the revolution was Colonel Gamal Abdel Nasser, since 1954 president and almost absolute ruler of Egypt.

163

With a largely illiterate population of close to thirty million, almost one and one-half the size of 1950, Egypt's most pressing problems are economic. Nasser hopes to solve these problems with his program of "Arab socialism"—land reform, development of natural resources, increased industrialization, and a more equitable distribution of wealth. Outstanding among his projects has been the construction of a gigantic dam and power station near Aswan on the Nile. The money for the project was originally to come from the United States and Great Britain; but when Nasser also asked for aid from the Communist bloc, which was already supplying him with arms, the Western powers in the summer of 1956 withdrew their offer. Nasser thereupon retaliated by nationalizing the Suez Canal, claiming that its income was needed to pay for the Aswan Dam. This act of defiance almost plunged the world into a major war, as Israel, followed by England and France, invaded Egypt. It was only due to quick United Nations action that peace was kept. The winner in the Suez crisis was President Nasser. The Suez Canal remained under Egyptian control, bringing in some one hundred and fifty million dollars worth of precious foreign currency each year. The Russians loaned Egypt the necessary funds to start the Aswan Dam, and in time the West, too, resumed its economic aid. Nasser thus emerged as one of the more unscrupulous neutralists, successfully playing one side against the other.

Nasser's successful dealings with the great powers of both East and West made him the natural leader of the Arab world. The Egyptian president initially had shown little interest in Pan-Arabism; but once he realized its possible advantages he became its most ardent prophet. A first and major step toward Arab unity was taken in 1958 when Egypt and Syria joined forces in the United Arab Republic (UAR) under the presidency of Nasser. The initiative for the UAR had come from Syria. When the advantages expected from such a union failed to materialize, however, Syria in 1961 broke away and resumed her independence. In the meantime Nasser's hopes of widening the UAR by including Jordan, Lebanon, and Iraq had failed. In Jordan youthful King Hussein took firm measures against Nasser's efforts to promote the overthrow of his regime. In Lebanon an insurrection of pro-Nasser partisans against the pro-American government in 1958 was foiled when some fifteen thousand United States marines temporarily occupied the country. The simultaneous overthrow of the pro-Western monarchy of Iraq at first was seen as a further step toward Arab unity. But the new regime of Abdul Karim Kassem refused to recognize Nasser's claim to leadership in the Arab world and instead resumed the bitter rivalry that had characterized past relations between Iraq and Egypt.

These various failures to create a United Arab Republic in fact as well as in name (Egypt continues to use the UAR title) did not discourage Nasser. Using the Cairo radio and press, he continued a constant propaganda barrage aimed at the widespread popular sentiment for Arab unity in all Arab countries. In 1962 Egypt sent troops to Yemen to support the revolutionary regime of the new "Yemeni Arab Republic." In the spring of 1963 coups d'état in Iraq and Syria brought to power the Arab Socialist Renaissance (Baath) Party in both countries. Among its goals was Arab unity, and soon discussions were under way for some kind of federation with Nasser as president. But this latest dream of Arab unity did not last long, as Nasser insisted on far closer integration under his leadership than Syria or Iraq were ready to grant. When the members of the Arab League met in 1964 to discuss possible measures against Israel's Jordan River project, there were many signs of amity, but none of unity. The only way in which such unity might come about would be for Egypt's "Arab socialism" to prove itself at home and to substantiate Nasser's claim to leadership, which thus far is largely based on emotional appeal.

The Arab states of North Africa other than Egypt, while not really part of the Middle East, nevertheless are more deeply involved in the events of that critical area than in the affairs of Africa. They all have won their freedom since World War II: Libya was released from UN trusteeship in 1951; Sudan became a republic in 1956; the same year both Morocco and Tunisia were granted full sovereignty by France; and Algeria, as we have seen, became independent in 1962. Economically all these nations depend heavily on foreign aid. In the past such aid has come chiefly from the United States. More recently the Communist bloc also has begun to do its part. Tunisia, under President Habib Bourguiba, is the most pro-Western nation of the region. Morocco's King Hassan II and Algeria's President Ahmed Ben Bella lean somewhat to the East. Both Libya and Sudan are officially neutral, but their people are attracted by Nasser's appeal to Arab nationalism.

The smallest country of the Middle East to become independent was the island of Cyprus. It belongs to the Middle East only geographically; its culture is a mixture of Greek and Turkish. After four years of violence between Greek and Turkish Cypriotes, in which the British mother country was caught in the middle, the Republic of Cyprus finally celebrated its independence in 1960. Archbishop Makarios, who had led the fight for independence, was elected president. The new nation remained within the Commonwealth, and Britain retained her military bases on Cyprus. Relations between Greek and Turkish Cypriotes, however, remained tense. Under the Cyprus constitution the Turkish minority, which is outnumbered by more than four to one, was guaranteed certain rights. Attempts on the part of the Makarios government to curtail these rights met with resistance from the Cypriote Turks and finally, late in 1963, led to civil war. The United Nations sent a peacemaking force to Cyprus and tried to mediate between the Greek and Turkish factions. The situation was complicated by the fact that Turkey began aiding her nationals on Cyprus, while Greece encouraged agitation among Greek Cypriotes for *enosis*, that is, union with Greece. The Makarios regime would like Cyprus to remain independent under the rule of the Greek Cypriote majority. The Soviet Union supports Makarios's position.

The Cyprus crisis thus threatens to make the Middle East another battlefield in the cold war. The West has made preparations for a possible showdown. To meet the threat of Communist expansion in the Middle East, Great Britain, Turkey, Iran, Iraq, and Pakistan in 1955 formed the Middle East Treaty Organization (METO), or Baghdad Pact. In 1957 the United States joined in the defense of the region with the proclamation of the "Eisenhower Doctrine," under which America promised armed assistance against Communist aggression to any nation in the Middle East that requested it. Finally in 1958, when the new regime of Abdul Karim Kassem took Iraq out of the Baghdad Pact, the United States joined the remaining members of METO in forming the Central Treaty Organization (CENTO) which, like its predecessor, aims to contain the spread of communism.

None of the Arab nations is part of any of these regional defense groupings. They all prefer to follow a neutralist course, partly for reasons of national pride, partly because they thus hope to gain aid from both East and West. If, nevertheless, some of the Arab nations seem more friendly toward the East, this may be explained by their past experiences with Western imperialism. Communism as such has been a problem only in Iraq. As a revolutionary force its importance has been overshadowed by nationalism. This does not mean that a closer affiliation between the Arab world and the Communist bloc would not seriously weaken the Western position in the cold war. To maintain what remains of Western influence in the Middle East, without further arousing Arab nationalism, is the difficult task of the Western powers at the present time.

TURBULENT AFRICA

The tide of colonial nationalism, after sweeping through Asia and the Middle East, finally also reached Africa. In 1950 there were still only four sovereign states on that vast continent. Fifteen years later their number had grown to thirty-six. With the remaining British colonies in Central and South Africa approaching independence or at least self-government, the only remnants of traditional colonialism in Africa today are the large Portuguese holdings in Portuguese Guinea, Angola, and Mozambique and the Spanish Sahara.

Most of the recent victories of African nationalism have been won in the hitherto least developed part of the continent south of the Sahara Desert. This region, abounding in natural resources, is inhabited by close to two hundred million Africans and about four million whites. Most of the latter live in the Republic of South Africa. The native peoples are still extremely backward, illiterate, and poor. Tropical diseases, thanks to the efforts of the former colonial powers, have been virtually stamped out, at least in the more densely populated areas. But the resultant population growth has far outrun the food supply, so that much of Africa is chronically undernourished. There is nowhere any tradition of political unity, the tribe having always been the largest unit of native life. And with some seven hundred different dialects there is no common language other than French or English. Diversity and complexity are the outstanding characteristics of the Dark Continent.

The only unifying force throughout Africa is nationalism. In its deep-seated distrust of the white man, African nationalism was not content with half-measures. It demanded complete and immediate independence, despite the fact that most Africans were hardly ready for it. This headlong rush into freedom has caused many difficulties. The way in which these are being solved depends

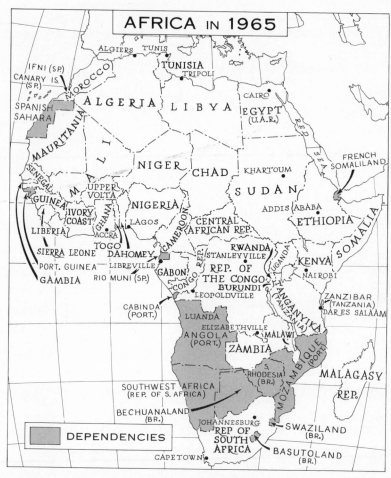

AFRICA IN 1965

DEPENDENCIES

not only on the natives but on the former colonial powers, because even though most of Africa today is nominally independent, the West still has a great deal of influence.

In only one African country today is a white minority trying to hold on tenaciously to a predominating European culture. The Republic of South Africa is ruled by its three million whites, who constitute about one-fifth of the total population. The nonwhite majority (Africans, Indians, and mixed) has been granted a few concessions; but these fall far short of the growing demand for full equality. In 1948 the South African government adopted a program of strict racial segregation, or *apartheid*. It aims at the complete separation of races, restriction of franchise for nonwhites, forced resettlement of Africans in rural areas, school segregation, and a lower educational standard for African children. The inferior status of the native is thus to be perpetuated by every possible means. The result has been mounting unrest, riots, and bloodshed. How much longer this repressive policy will succeed is impossible to say. Meanwhile the attempt to reverse by force the inevitable trend toward racial equality has earned South Africa the censure of most of the civilized world. Opposition to South Africa's racial policy by other Commonwealth members led to her withdrawal from the Commonwealth in 1961.

There are other regions in Africa where white minorities continue to wield disproportionate influence; but outside forces are at work to change this situation. Portuguese colonialism finds itself under increasing attack from the free African states who use the United Nations Security Council as a means of censuring Portugal. In Southern Rhodesia, still formally a British dependency, independence is being withheld by the mother country until the white settlers grant political equality to the region's large African majority. Everywhere else in Africa transition from white to colored rule has been completed, and, with the exception of the former Belgian Congo, this transition has been peaceful and orderly. The French and particularly the British had for years past prepared their colonial peoples for self-government. Most of their former colonies are still members of the French Community or the (British) Commonwealth, and French and British citizens are active in their administration, education, and economic development. Such fruitful cooperation between whites and blacks holds the best promise for orderly evolution in Africa.

The new African states are so radically different in size, resources, and stage of growth that any valid generalizations about them are impossible. Some, like the Congo, have an abundance of natural riches; others, like Somalia, Mali, or Mauritania, have none. Among the most viable states, aside from the Congo, are Nigeria, Ghana, Tanzania, and Kenya. They have important minerals, fertile soil, potential waterpower, and—in Nigeria and Ghana at least—a high rate of literacy. Nigeria in particular has made remarkable progress since gaining independence in 1960 and shows the best promise of becoming ultimately self-sustaining.

All African countries nominally are democracies, but lack of political experience, general backwardness of the population, and a long tradition of tribal disunity have prevented democracy from taking root. In some countries the trend has been toward a one-party state and the emergence of strong leaders like Kwame Nkrumah of Ghana, Julius Nyerere of Tanzania and Jomo Kenyatta of Kenya. At least one of them, Nkrumah, has used his position to become a dictator at home and a bully abroad.

The nation that has caused more international trouble than any other African state is the Republic of the Congo. One-third the size of the United States and with some sixteen million natives, it is one of the richest countries of Africa. The Belgians, during their seventy-five-year rule, did much to develop the region's economy, but too little to train the Congolese for self-government. This has been one of the main sources of the Congo's troubles. When the French in 1959 gave independence to their own Congo Republic, riots in the Belgian Congo made the Belgians give way far too quickly and set free their own prize possession. The Republic of the Congo under Premier Patrice Lumumba was established on June 30, 1960.

Events since then have demonstrated the error of Belgium's precipitate action. Within hours after independence the Congolese army mutinied and the Congolese people rioted. As the whites began fleeing the country, order broke down completely. Premier Lumumba, a high-strung and erratic young man, blamed everything on the Belgians and asked the United Nations to force the withdrawal of Belgian troops. A UN Emergency Force finally succeeded in getting the Belgians out. But this did not solve the Congo problem. In the interim strong opposition to Lumumba's high-handed policy had arisen among some of the Congo's six provinces, notably Kasai and Katanga. In September, 1960, the Congo's president, Joseph Kasavubu, with the aid of the army under Colonel Joseph Mobutu, removed Lumumba, charging him with creating chaos and showing pro-Communist leanings.

The removal of Lumumba and his subsequent murder, however, merely increased the confusion in the new state. In August, 1961, a certain measure of unity was achieved when the moderate Cyrille Adoula was elected premier. The one major source of trouble continued to be the wealthy Katanga province, where President Moise Tshombe insisted on pursuing an independent course. Katanga's secession was not ended until 1963, and then chiefly due to continued intervention of United Nations troops. But now new revolts against the central government at Leopoldville broke out in two other provinces, Kwilu and Kivu. When the Adoula government was unable to cope with these rebels, President Kasavubu, who by now had emerged as the nation's chief executive rather than a mere figurehead, appointed Moise Tshombe to succeed Adoula in July, 1964. It remained to be seen if the shrewd and resourceful Tshombe would succeed where so many before him had failed in bringing together the Congo's many dissident factions. The withdrawal of United Nations forces from the Congo, meanwhile, had removed one of the most important stabilizing factors in that faction-ridden country.

The solution of the Congo crisis was made more difficult because of the support which rebel forces everywhere received from the Communist world. The Soviet Union supported Lumumba and consistently opposed United Nations intervention. More recently Red China has taken a hand in fomenting trouble in the Congo and elsewhere, notably in Zanzibar. There is as yet no strong Communist movement in Africa. Only in the Republic of South Africa has there been a vigorous Communist underground. One of the most effective antidotes to communism is seen in a healthy trade-union movement. The beginnings of such a movement in Africa exist and deserve Western support. Still more important as a protection against communism is economic aid. More and more of it is given to Africa each year. But such aid must be without any political or military strings, because if there is one thing on which all the new nations of Africa agree, it is their desire to be rid of foreign influence. Neutralism is a potent force throughout the whole continent.

THE AFRO-ASIAN BLOC

The road to independence in the former colonial regions of Asia and Africa differed from country to country, depending on the attitudes of the colonial powers and on the degree of maturity of the native peoples concerned. Yet there were also certain similarities of problems and experiences to suggest some kind of collaboration among the many nations that had so recently won their freedom. Most of them, moreover, felt that by working together their influence on questions affecting them all might be stronger. It was these considerations that led to several conferences, both among the nations of Asia and Africa and among the African nations alone.

The first Asian-African Congress met at Bandung, Indonesia, in 1955. Twenty-nine countries participated, representing about half the world's population. As was to be expected from so large and diverse a gathering, the specific achievements of the conference were few. But as far as establishing a common attitude on basic issues was concerned, the meeting was a success. The members agreed overwhelmingly in their condemnation of colonialism, advocacy of universal membership in the United Nations, and censure of racial discrimination. Discussion throughout the conference was on a high level and free from any bitterness against the white powers.

The same could not be said for the next meeting, the Afro-Asian People's Solidarity Conference, which convened at Cairo in 1957. It was an unofficial assemblage of peoples rather than governments and was attended by representatives from forty countries, including Russia and the Asian members of the Communist bloc. Under the subtle instigation of the Soviet Union its deliberations and resolutions followed a clearly Communist line. The Russians used the occasion to make vague but impressive promises of "stringless" aid to African and Asian countries and to attack "Western imperialism." There were similar Solidarity Conferences in 1960 and 1963. By that time the majority of the delegates were Communist or pro-Communist. The tenor of all meetings was strongly anti-Western. A series of Afro-Asian Economic Conferences between 1958 and 1963 was less Communist-dominated and more businesslike. The first meeting voted to exclude the Soviet Union, since it did not belong to the Afro-Asian family. The delegates also founded the Afro-Asian Organization for Economic Cooperation to explore ways in which its members could aid each other economically. Another intercontinental meeting, including not only Asian and African states but also Yugoslavia and some South American countries, was the Conference of Nonaligned States which met in Cairo in 1962 to discuss common economic problems. Its final resolution pointed out that underdeveloped countries must try to help themselves as well as look for aid from the more highly developed nations. A similar gathering of some fifty-seven nonaligned nations took place in 1964, again in Cairo, calling for peaceful coexistence, self-determination, elimination of foreign bases, and nuclear disarmament.

In 1958 the nations of Africa founded their own Conference of Independent African States which held annual meetings thereafter. The Union of South Africa was excluded from all such meetings, and its racial policy was condemned in the strongest terms. Similar protests were launched against Portugal for holding on to her large African colonies. The proceedings were usually statesmanlike and free from anti-Western tirades. These were reserved for the All-African Peoples' Conference, a gathering of unofficial delegations which first met in 1958 and again in 1960 and 1961. Here the Western powers were sharply criticized for their "neo-colonialism," that is, their alleged efforts to perpetuate their former influence indirectly. Greetings sent to the Peoples' Conferences from the Soviet Union and Communist China were invariably applauded, while similar greetings from the United States were greeted with silence. More constructive work was done by the UN-sponsored Economic Commission for Africa (ECA), which was created in 1958 and has held several meetings since. France, Great Britain, and Belgium are among the members, and the United States and Russia are represented by observers.

As more and more African states won their independence, the need arose for some closer cooperation, especially in the economic field. The result was a number of regional federations and associations that developed in the early 1960's. The former British territories established the Pan-African Freedom Movement of East and Central Africa; the former French colonies created the African and Malgache Union; some of the new states in northern Africa formed a group known as the "Casablanca powers"; and Morocco, Algeria, and Tunisia worked toward a Maghreb Union. There were several other such groupings. The next step, obviously, was to create a wider union including all of Africa. But here disagreement soon arose over the degree of integration such a union should achieve. President Nkrumah of Ghana was the leading advocate of a strong federation of African states. He was opposed by most other African leaders who suspected Nkrumah of seeking to extend his authoritarian rule beyond the borders of Ghana. The issue was aired at every meeting of African states without making any progress. Finally, in May, 1963, a Summit Conference on African Unity was convened in Addis Ababa, Ethiopia.

The result of the conference was the formation of the Organization of African Unity (OAU). Its Charter calls for annual meetings of African heads of state and for biannual meetings of their foreign ministers. It also established a permanent Secretariat with headquarters at Addis Ababa. The first secretary general, appointed in 1964, was a Guinean diplomat, Diallo Telli Boubacar. The main purpose of the OAU is to serve as a permanent framework for economic and political cooperation among African states. As such it has presented a common African front in the United Nations on such issues as South Africa and Portugal. An African Liberation Committee under the OAU seeks "to help oppressed people to achieve speedy, effective independence." The OAU has actively supported native revolts in the Portuguese colonies, and it has successfully mediated a number of border disputes among member states. While the OAU has been united in its opposition to colonialism, it has shown far less agreement on the question of African unity. This was shown at the Organization's first annual meeting in Cairo in 1964. Speeches and resolutions condemning "imperialism" and "neo-colonialism" were widely applauded, but so was a blistering attack by President Nyerere of Tanzania against Nkrumah's demands for a United States of Africa. An all-African union, it seems, is at best a very distant possibility.

Africa's preoccupation with its own affairs in recent years has come to overshadow the earlier efforts at Afro-Asian collaboration. One place where such collaboration continues to be important is in the United Nations. Since 1963 the Afro-Asian bloc has commanded a majority of seats in the UN General Assembly. It is only natural that the new states should demand a more important voice in UN affairs. The African-Asian group has already been given more posts in the UN Secretariat whose head, U Thant, is himself an Asian. Efforts to gain increased representation on the Security Council, either by redistributing the existing seats or by creating additional ones, are under way. These changes will necessarily make the UN far different from what it started out to be twenty years ago. Yet just as the African states continue to disagree among each other over African issues, so do the African and Asian states disagree over many larger international issues. Most of the Asian states have been independent for a decade or more and take a far less radical view of colonialism than some of the younger states of Africa. The "rising tide of color," feared by many in the West, is very much a reality today. This does not mean, however, that it must lead to racial violence. The more responsible leaders in Asia and Africa are aware of the danger and futility of racial intolerance. They realize that, just as their countries could not have reached their present state of development without colonialism, so they will not be able to solve their remaining problems without continued aid from the former colonial powers. The problem of the underdeveloped countries is a joint responsibility of the whole civilized world and the greatest challenge of our era of competitive coexistence.

6

FRIENDLY COMPETITORS

Competitive coexistence, though tough, can also be
friendly, as shown in the picture of
American Astronaut John Glenn and Soviet Cosmonaut
Gherman Titov during the latter's visit to
the United States in 1962.   WIDE WORLD PHOTOS.

COMPETITIVE
COEXISTENCE

THE COLD WAR, AS WE HAVE SEEN, DID NOT break out overnight. It came as the result of a gradually mounting crisis between the East and West, in which action by one side usually brought on an equally strong reaction by the other (see Chapter 1). As both parties perfected their nuclear arsenals, however, mutual distrust gave way to fear of mutual annihilation. It was in this atmosphere that the idea of coexistence emerged, not as an alternative to cold war, but as a prolonged armistice in that war. The hope that two such diametrically opposed systems as the free, democratic West and the authoritarian, Communist East might exist peacefully side by side was nothing new. Such hope had guided American policy at the end of the World War II and had led to most of the concessions that were made to the Russians at that time. Once Americans had awakened to the continued threat of world communism, however, they had drastically changed their attitude. Instead of idealizing the Soviet Union as a wartime ally, they now saw communism in its true light as the free world's greatest enemy. The majority of America's allies at first approved of and shared this changed attitude. Only when the terrible consequences of a possible nuclear war were realized by western Europeans did they become restive under United States leadership and begin to criticize American foreign policy.

ALLIED CRITICISM OF
THE UNITED STATES

Such Allied criticism was part of a general decline in American popularity abroad. The story of how this decline came about is complicated. Much of it was due to circumstances beyond American control, such as the emergence of new regimes capitalizing on Communist-inspired anti-Americanism, or the resentment of peoples growing tired of seeing American soldiers in their midst, be they occupation troops or allies. Then there was the element of envy on the part of countries still caught in postwar austerity toward a nation so obviously affluent. Yet there were also certain American policies which caused uneasiness abroad. Many Europeans feared that the United States might once more turn isolationist and concentrate on the military defense and economic development of the Western Hemisphere. Measures like the Mc-Carran-Walter Act, which restricted immigration into the United States, or America's refusal to ease its trade relations by lowering tariff barriers were interpreted as signs of a new American nationalism. "McCarthyism," which antagonized many of America's best friends, was seen as a further sign.

Nobody could deny, of course, that the United States showed an increasing awareness of its new responsibilities as a world power. The manner in which America executed this leadership, however, left much to be desired in the opinion of foreign critics. The most common criticism was that America during the cold war emphasized military aid at the expense of economic assistance. In her search for allies, furthermore, America was accused of a lack of discrimination by favoring such former or present Fascist nations as Germany, Japan, and Spain. Occasional threats that the United States might withdraw its military forces or its economic aid from Europe if its allies failed to do as they were told were seen as signs of isolationism or of unwarranted interference in the affairs of other nations. The particular target of this foreign criticism was America's Secretary of State John Foster Dulles. Dulles had stressed the need for an "agonizing reappraisal" of his country's foreign policy in the light of American self-interest; he had threatened "utilizing the deterrence of massive retaliation" by atomic weapons at times and places of America's choosing; and he had spoken of "rolling back" the iron curtain by encouraging rebellion among the Soviet satellites. Such blunt utterances were felt to be careless and irresponsible, since they might involve everyone in what Arnold Toynbee called "annihilation without representation."

America's intransigence toward the Russians was deplored particularly at a time when, following the death of Stalin in 1953, the leaders in the Kremlin proclaimed a "new course" in Soviet domestic and foreign affairs. As usual the United States was far more reluctant than its allies to accept the Soviet Union's peaceful declarations at face value. To strike a positive note, President Eisenhower, in December, 1953, put before the United Nations his "atoms for peace" plan. He urged the powers to cooperate in developing peacetime uses of atomic energy, and he suggested the donation of fissionable materials to an international pool in order to aid peaceful atomic development. The calming effect of this generous scheme, however, was obliterated shortly afterwards by Secretary Dulles' statement on "massive retaliation."

THE SEARCH FOR COEXISTENCE

Given America's continued suspicion of the Soviet Union, the search for a basis of possible coexistence was a slow process. The fact that the Big Four foreign ministers, after an interlude of several years, resumed their talks at a conference in Berlin in early 1954 was a hopeful sign. Another important meeting, this one devoted to Far Eastern affairs, took place in the spring of 1954 at Geneva. With nineteen nations attending, the novel feature of the Geneva Conference was the presence, for the first time at such a meeting, of Communist China. The main objectives of the talks were to reunite Korea (where an armistice had been reached the year before) and to end the fighting in Indochina. Although the efforts with respect to Korea failed, the powers did temporarily restore peace to Indochina (see p. 156). It was while the Geneva Conference was still in session that the Western leaders made their first open declarations that echoed Russia's proposals for peaceful coexistence. In June, 1954, Winston Churchill, whose "iron curtain" speech in 1946 had sounded the start of the cold war, publicly advocated "a try for peaceful coexistence—a real good try." Two days later President Eisenhower gave qualified approval to Churchill's views when he agreed that the East and West must "find ways of living together."

The result of this apparent willingness of East and West to find some modus vivendi was the "meeting at the summit" in the summer of 1955. The year got off to a bad start when the Chinese Communists seized some of the smaller Nationalist-held islands between Formosa and the Chinese mainland. For several weeks it appeared as if war between the United States (supporting Chiang Kai-shek) and Red China was inevitable, especially as the latter began threatening the key islands of Matsu and Quemoy. But by late April the Communists suddenly became more moderate and agreed to solve the problems of the Formosa Strait, by negotiation. There was a similar relaxation of tension in Europe. In May, 1955, the Soviet Union suddenly declared its readiness to sign an Austrian peace treaty on reasonable terms (see p. 60). In view of these and other indications of Communist moderation, the moment seemed auspicious to hold a top-level conference between Eastern and Western leaders. The meeting between President Eisenhower, Premier Bulganin, Prime Minister Eden, and Premier Faure took place in Geneva in July, 1955.

This was the first meeting of the Big Four since the Potsdam Conference ten years earlier. The atmosphere of the discussions was cordial, and the "spirit of Geneva" tended to obscure, for the moment at least, the continued differences between the two camps. The conference dealt with four main subjects: German reunification, European security, disarmament, and the improvement of East-West relations. On none of these topics except the last did the powers reach any agreement. The first two points were closely related, since Soviet opposition to German reunification was allegedly based on the fear that a reunified and rearmed Germany would pose a threat to European security. The three Western leaders placed the German issue first, calling for immediate free elections to bring about reunification. To meet Russian fears of possible German aggression, they were willing to consider some general European security plan, a partial limitation of armaments, and a demilitarized area between the East and West. The Russians, on the other hand, were afraid that free German elections would result in a Communist defeat and insisted that European security should take precedence over German reunification. The Soviet negotiators, among them Khrushchev, proposed the dissolution of NATO and of its Eastern counterpart, the Warsaw Pact, and the substitution of an all-European security system that would include the United States. This last concession became meaningless, however, when the Russians also called for the ultimate withdrawal of all non-European forces.

Similar divergence of views existed on the issue of disarmament. President Eisenhower again stressed the need for effective control as the first step in any disarmament plan. The President suggested that the U.S.S.R. and the United States exchange complete blueprints of their military establishments and permit unlimited aerial inspection to check on hidden concentrations of arms. The Russians refused to accept this "open skies" proposal. Instead they insisted that a ban on all nuclear weapons precede any system of inspection. The only subject on which agreement was reached, at least in principle, concerned the desirability of improving economic and cultural relations between the East and West.

Despite a spirit of genuine friendliness the accomplishments of the Geneva Conference were small indeed. Yet the summit meeting actually seemed to have improved the international climate. In August, 1955, an International Conference on the Peaceful Uses of Atomic Energy at Geneva brought together scientists from the Communist and free worlds for the first time in twenty years to exchange information. In September the Russians caused a pleasant surprise when they announced their readiness to withdraw from Finland's Porkkala Peninsula (see p. 15). Exchange visits by Russian and Western teams of experts and an increased flow of tourists across the iron curtain were seen as further signs that East-West relations had really changed. But there were also indications that the change did not go very deep. When Chancellor Adenauer visited Moscow in September, 1955, to discuss the establishment of diplomatic relations between the Soviet Union and the German Federal Republic, he was told that West Germany's membership in NATO was the main obstacle to German reunification. Shortly thereafter the Soviet government reaffirmed the legitimacy of the East German Communist regime and the permanence of Germany's eastern frontiers, as established at Potsdam (see

p. 11,). About this same time the West was troubled by the news of an arms deal between Czechoslovakia and Egypt, which showed the Communist intention of trying to meddle in the affairs of the Middle East. At the tenth session of the UN General Assembly in September Secretary of State Dulles once again crossed verbal swords with Foreign Minister Molotov. Such signs of continued East-West tension did not augur well for the Geneva Conference of the Big Four's foreign ministers that took place to follow up the summit meeting in October and November, 1955.

The foreign ministers, taking up once again the issues discussed three months earlier, did not come any closer to agreement. On the tangled issue of Germany the Russians now proposed that reunification should be brought about through agreement between the two German regimes. The disarmament discussions again foundered on Russia's refusal to agree to any effective plan of mutual inspection. As for improving economic and cultural relations between the East and West, the Russians rejected Western requests to permit Russian citizens to travel freely outside Russia, to abolish censorship within the Soviet Union, and to reduce trade barriers. All in all the efforts of the foreign ministers came to nothing. As the conference proceeded, it lost all traces of the cordiality that had prevailed at the summit meeting and again displayed the spirit of bitter recrimination that had prevailed at all earlier conferences.

THE COLD WAR CONTINUES

The search for peaceful coexistence by way of a settlement of East-West differences had thus failed. For a while the lull in the cold war continued. In January, 1956, Soviet Premier Bulganin, in a letter to President Eisenhower, offered the United States a twenty-year treaty of friendship and cooperation. The President, however, objected that such a treaty might "work against the cause of peace by creating the illusion that a stroke of the pen had achieved a result which, in fact, can be obtained only by a change of spirit." Such a change of spirit, it seemed, was actually under way. Khrushchev's denouncement of Stalin at the Twentieth Party Congress, the announcement of a drastic cut in Soviet armed forces, and the Khrushchev-Tito declaration endorsing "different roads to socialism" in different countries, all were seen as hopeful signs that Russia's leaders were sincere in their advocacy of a "new course" at home and abroad.

At this point events in Hungary and the Middle East dashed all such hopes. Russia's role during the Suez crisis was mainly one of fanning the flames of Arab nationalism. By supporting Egypt throughout, Moscow not only won Nasser's gratitude, but was able to pose as a champion of anticolonialism in the eyes of Asians and Africans. Russia's gain in the Middle East, however, was offset by the loss of face she suffered because of her intervention in Hungary. The UN General Assembly condemned the Soviet Union for depriving the Hungarians of their freedom, and in this action even some of the neutralist nations concurred. While Russia's prestige was shaken, the influence and popularity of the United States remained high. With the proclamation of the Eisenhower Doctrine in early 1957, America served notice that she was ready to challenge the spread of Soviet influence in the Middle East. The Russians continued to sound the coexistence note. "There have been many cases of marriages without love where people get along," Khrushchev said in 1957. "Let us do it—without love, but getting on together." After what had happened in 1956, Americans could hardly be blamed for being suspicious of any such "marriage of convenience."

There were no major international crises in 1957. Nevertheless it was a crucial year in the cold war. The most important developments occurred within the Soviet Union. In July, 1957, Khrushchev won his victory over the "anti-party" group in the Presidium, emerging as the supreme voice of communism. A month later Russia announced the successful test of an intercontinental ballistic missile. While the West remained skeptical of Soviet claims to leadership in the missile field, the Russians on October 4, 1957, launched their first earth satellite, Sputnik I. The successful launching of a second satellite, weighing half a ton, proved beyond any doubt that the Soviet Union possessed rockets powerful enough to deliver a nuclear warhead over an intercontinental distance. The failure of America's effort to launch her own test satellite in December, 1957, merely underlined the fact that the Russians held a substantial lead in a field in which the United States had always been thought superior. The balance of power in the cold war had suddenly and dramatically shifted to Russia's advantage.

The result of this shift was confusion in the West and a stiffening of attitude in the East. America's allies urged that ways be found to check the arms race by negotiating with the Russians. The disarmament plan most widely discussed at the time was one of "disengagement." Its main advocate was Poland's Foreign Minister Adam Rapacki. He proposed a ban on the production of nuclear weapons and their elimination from central Europe (East and West Germany, Poland, and Czechoslovakia), followed by a reduction and separation of military forces in that critical area. The Russians advanced several versions of such disengagement schemes, and similar proposals were made in the West. But the United States suspected that Russia's motives were not so much to lessen tension as to weaken NATO. America launched her first satellite, Explorer I, in January, 1958. The Russians maintained their lead by putting their far bigger one-and-one-half-ton Sputnik III into orbit. At the same time they made free with vague but high-sounding proposals intended to make them appear as champions of peace. When asked to come to grips with specific issues of the cold war, however, the Russians refused to commit themselves.

Besides waging a diplomatic offensive against the West, the Communists were also responsible for several serious international crises in 1958. In the Middle East they supported President Nasser in his drive to unify the Arab world. When the United States and Great Britain sent troops to Lebanon and Jordan, respectively, to protect these nations against Nasser, the move was denounced by Soviet Foreign Minister Andrei Gromyko as "unprovoked intervention" stemming from greed for oil. Next came the crisis in the Far East, where Chinese Communist attacks on Quemoy and Matsu brought on a war scare which was resolved only by America's firmness in protecting Nationalist Chinese convoys to the offshore islands. The most irresponsible act of throwing the world into a state of fear was Premier Khrushchev's announcement in November, 1958, that the Soviet Union no longer recognized the occupation rights of the Western powers in West Berlin. France, Britain, and the United States flatly rejected this latest Communist challenge, but the Soviet leader remained firm, setting a six-month deadline after which West Berlin would become a "free city." By challenging the Western position in Berlin, Khrushchev hoped to reopen the German question. When the Communists discovered, however, that their policy of threats, far from weakening, actually strengthened and united the free world, they decided once again on a more conciliatory approach. In January, 1959, Krushchev's righthand man, First Deputy Premier Anastas I. Mikoyan, during a tour of the United States urged an early summit meeting to settle major East-West differences. In July President Eisenhower's right-hand man, Vice-President Nixon, on a visit to Russia called for "increasing the contacts between the leaders and peoples of our two countries." In August, 1959, plans were announced for an exchange of visits between President Eisenhower and Premier Khrushchev.

The Russian leader came to the United States in September, 1959, and stayed for ten days. During that time he traveled widely and talked freely. The high point of the visit came during the last two days, which Khrushchev spent as President Eisenhower's guest at the latter's retreat in Camp David. The major topics discussed by the two men and their advisers were Berlin and disarmament. On neither of them did they reach any agreement. Negotiations on Berlin were to be reopened later, but without the time limit on which Khrushchev had insisted earlier. As for disarmament the two leaders agreed to "make every effort to achieve a constructive solution." The chief gain from the Camp David discussions was the personal contact they permitted between the world's two most powerful men. President Eisenhower afterwards described Khrushchev as "an extraordinary personality"; and Khrushchev praised the President's "wise statesmanship." The "spirit of Camp David," like the "spirit of Geneva" four years earlier, became the byword for what was expected to be a new phase in East-West relations.

SUMMIT MEETINGS THAT FAILED

One of the results of the Eisenhower-Khrushchev talks was to ease the way toward another summit meeting. Prime Minister Macmillan of Great Britain had long favored such a meeting, feeling that as long as the East and West "kept talking" the danger of war would be minimized. The United States, now that Premier Khrushchev had lifted the time limit on the Berlin issue, also was ready to give the summit a try. The only resistance came from President de Gaulle of France, who wanted a conference on issues much wider than Berlin and disarmament, and who insisted that a summit meeting needed careful, long-range preparation. It was De Gaulle's approach that prevailed. The second "meeting at the summit" was not held until the spring of 1960. The interim was taken up with prolonged negotiations within the Western camp to decide on an agenda for the conference. While no formal list was prepared, it was generally understood that the summit would deal with the problems of Germany and Berlin, disarmament, and the relaxation of East-West tensions. These points, it will be noted, were similar to the ones that had been discussed at the first summit meeting in 1955 and at almost every East-West meeting before and since.

While the Western Allies were getting ready to present a united front at the summit, President Eisenhower and Premier Khrushchev went on extended goodwill tours to proclaim the peaceful intentions of their countries and to win the sympathy of the neutral nations for their respective causes. The President in late 1959 traveled some twenty-two thousand miles, visiting eleven countries. Wherever he went, he was given a warm reception. Not to be outdone, Premier Khrushchev went on the road in early 1960. He traveled only twelve thousand miles, but he had already covered twice that distance during the previous six months. His reception, while friendly, did not compare with the welcome given President Eisenhower. From various Soviet statements during the spring of 1960, it seemed unlikely that the Russians were ready to make any major concessions on the issues separating the East and West. Still there was always the hope that once Khrushchev met the Western leaders face to face, some limited progress toward agreement might be made.

The summit conference was scheduled for mid-May, 1960, in Paris. Two weeks before the delegates assembled, the Russians downed an American U-2 plane engaged in an intelligence mission over the Soviet Union. This was the seventeenth incident in ten years involving United States planes, most of them flying near rather than over Russian territory. While on earlier occasions the Russians had been satisfied with making diplomatic protests, this time they decided to make a major issue out of American "espionage." Premier Khrushchev, in breaking the news of the U-2 incident, saw little hope any longer for the success of the summit meeting. He later warned that he would use rockets against any country that lent its bases to future United States flights over the U.S.S.R., and that such flights would lead to war. American authorities at first denied that they had sent the U-2 plane on its mission but later had to reverse their stand. Such clumsiness cast serious doubts on America's leadership. As a result, predictions about the outcome of the Paris conference were pessimistic.

As it turned out, the summit meeting never really got under way. At its opening session on May 16, 1960, Khrushchev launched into a savage attack on the United States and President Eisenhower who, he said, would no longer be welcome if he came to Russia. Khrushchev demanded that the President apologize for the U-2 incident and that those persons guilty of "deliberate violation of the Soviet Union" be punished. When these demands were rejected, the Russian leader left Paris. The West, in a joint communiqué, blamed the failure of the summit meeting on Khrushchev. The Russians in turn accused the United States of torpedoing the conference by aggressive actions.

The summit fiasco did not noticeably affect cold-war tensions, which had been running high for some time. Soviet Foreign Minister Gromyko, in a vain attempt to have the UN Security Council condemn the U-2 flight as "aggressive," called America's action "bandit-like" and "piratical." In early July the Russian delegation walked out of the UN Disarmament Commission in Geneva, charging that the West was not negotiating in good faith. Not long afterwards Premier Khrushchev threatened to use intercontinental missiles if the United States made any attempt to intervene against Castro in Cuba. The intensity of this new Soviet offensive in the cold war caused anxiety and bewilderment in the West. "I simply do not understand what is your purpose," British Prime Minister Macmillan wrote Khrushchev in a direct appeal to reason. Some Western observers suspected that Khrushchev's new toughness was due to pressure from Communist China. The heavy sacrifices involved in China's "great leap," it was felt, would be borne more readily by the Chinese people if these sacrifices were necessary to win the cold war. Peaceful coexistence implied a degree of mutual tolerance between capitalism and communism which was alien to strict Marxian doctrine. Instead, the Chinese Communists asserted that lasting peace would come only as the result of a class struggle against capitalism and imperialism. Western imperialism was still the favorite target of Soviet and Chinese Communists alike. Soviet actions in backing Fidel Castro in Cuba and Patrice Lumumba in the Congo were defended on grounds of anti-imperialism, as were Communist attempts to undermine America's position in the Far East, especially in Japan.

In June, 1960, President Eisenhower went on a goodwill tour of America's allies in the Far East. With one major exception he was given a rousing welcome everywhere. The exception was Japan.

There the announcement of President Eisenhower's trip caused such violently hostile demonstrations that his visit had to be canceled. At the root of the trouble was the agitation of a determined, Communist-led minority against a new United States–Japanese security treaty to replace the one signed in 1951. Despite Soviet warnings of "dangerous consequences" the new agreement was finally ratified. Even so, the failure of President Eisenhower to visit Japan was a serious blow to American prestige and a victory for communism.

In the fall of 1960 the theater of the cold war shifted briefly to the halls of the United Nations in New York. In an attempt to use the United Nations as a forum for his propaganda line Premier Krushchev attended the Fifteenth General Assembly. He brought with him several of his minions from eastern Europe, and while in New York he found an additional ally in his latest friend, Cuba's Fidel Castro. To present the case for the West, President Eisenhower and Prime Minister Macmillan put in brief appearances. The leading neutralist nations were represented by Tito of Yugoslavia, Nasser of the United Arab Republic, Nkrumah of Ghana, Nehru of India, and Sukarno of Indonesia. Also present were the heads of state of several smaller countries, including most of the new African states. Never before had the United Nations played host to so many illustrious delegates. Here, in effect, was another kind of "summit meeting."

For nearly four weeks the spotlight was on the bewildering antics of Premier Khrushchev. Alternating between threats and cajolery, he tried to dominate proceedings by appealing for support of the neutralists. In doing so he treated the Assembly to a series of performances never before witnessed in this decorous body—insulting and heckling delegates, calling the Security Council a spittoon and the Secretary General a fool, and taking off his shoe for use as a gavel. Orderly democratic procedure was obviously alien to the Russian leader. In the course of these goings-on, some old and several new issues came up for debate. Disarmament again occupied the center of the stage, but no agreement was reached. All in all, the results of the UN summit meeting were a draw, each side having made some gains and sustained some losses. The United Nations had increased its prestige, but hardly its power, and the two superpowers as usual had dominated the proceedings.

TO THE BRINK OF WAR

For a brief moment in early 1961 there was hope that the change of administration in Washington might bring a decrease of East-West tension. President Kennedy had inherited a heavy load of foreign troubles from his predecessor, and it was not long before his government faced its first major crisis in the abortive Cuban invasion of April, 1961. Premier Khrushchev had found some cordial words for the young President, and Kennedy had repeatedly expressed his readiness to join the Russian leader in pushing back "the jungle of suspicion" and establishing "a beachhead of co-operation." An opportunity for thus ironing out East-West differences came in June, 1961, when the two men met briefly on neutral ground in Vienna. President Kennedy hoped that he could get the Soviet premier to call off the Berlin crisis and that they might reach agreement on some other cold-war issues, especially a nuclear test ban treaty. But the Vienna meeting, while "useful" and "courteous," was also "somber" and "disappointing." The Russians, who just recently had sent their first man into orbit, were in no mood to make concessions. But at least, as President Kennedy said when he returned from Vienna, "the chances of a dangerous misjudgment on either side should be less," now that the two leaders had met and taken each other's measure. As far as Khrushchev was concerned this, unfortunately, was not true.

Shortly after the Vienna meeting the Russians stepped up their agitation over Berlin, threatening to sign a peace treaty with East Germany and to turn over the control of the access routes to West Berlin to the East Germans. To stop the flood of refugees from East Germany into West Berlin, the Communists in August, 1961, built the shameful Berlin wall which made East Germany into a huge prison. The United States protested and sent some token military reinforcements to West Berlin, but that was all. A few weeks later the Soviet Union broke the self-imposed nuclear test ban which the major powers had adhered to since 1958 and started on a fresh round of atomic explosions. The West pleaded in vain for a ban on above-ground nuclear tests to check the danger from radioactive fallout. In order not to fall too far behind in the nuclear race, the United States resumed its own testing in April, 1962. Meanwhile there had been some slight easing of tension when the Soviets abandoned their latest Berlin deadline and agreed to continue negotiations on the Berlin issue. A further positive achievement was seen in the Geneva accord on Laos in July 1962, which was expected to calm the situation in Southeast Asia. But all this time the Soviet Union was engaged in secret activities in Cuba that were to bring the United States and the Soviet Union closer to the brink of war than at any time since 1945.

The Cuban crisis developed gradually during the summer of 1962, as reports reached Washington that Castro was building up his military strength with the aid of Soviet equipment and technicians. By mid-October the United States had proof that this equipment included missiles and bombers capable of delivering nuclear weapons, and that Cuban missile sites and airfields were under construction. President Kennedy informed the American people of this situation in a speech on October 22. At the same time he imposed a strict quarantine upon arms shipments to Cuba, to be enforced by the United States navy and air force. While the Soviet Union challenged America's right to quarantine and accused the United States of fomenting nuclear war, the United States took its demand for the dismantling of the Cuban missile bases to the United Nations. A few Russian ships bound for Cuba were stopped by American warships, but there were no serious incidents. Premier Khrushchev, faced with determined American resistance and UN pressure, agreed to withdraw all Soviet offensive weapons from Cuba if the United States would remove her own such weapons from Turkey. When President Kennedy stood firm, the Russian leader gave in, insisting merely on an American pledge not to invade Cuba. When that pledge was given, Soviet missiles and installations were dismantled and shipped back to the Soviet Union. The whole crisis was over in less than two weeks.

THE THAW IN THE COLD WAR

The Cuban crisis, far from intensifying the cold war, ushered in the first genuine thaw in the East-West conflict. The Soviet Union and the United States continued to be on opposite sides in almost every crisis anywhere in the world, of course, from Indochina to Cyprus, and from the Congo to Indonesia; but there were fewer direct clashes and confrontations. It seemed as though the sudden threat of a nuclear holocaust had had a decidedly sobering effect upon both sides. In June, 1963, the two countries signed an agreement establishing an emergency "hot line" of direct communication between Washington and Moscow to reduce the risk of accidental war. In September President Kennedy, in a speech to the United Nations, suggested that America and Russia combine forces in a joint expedition to the moon. A month later the United States agreed to sell the Russians some two hundred fifty million dollars' worth of American surplus wheat. These small signs of relaxation did not extend to more basic issues like Berlin, Germany, or disarmament. President Kennedy and President Johnson after him made perfectly plain their continued insistence on Western presence in Berlin and on ultimate unification of Germany through free elections. The Russians, on the other hand, asserted their own position by occasionally halting an Allied convoy on the road to West Berlin. In the disarmament negotiations, as we shall see, disagreement continued on a number of points, notably inspection. Only on one minor aspect of disarmament—the ban on nuclear testing—was some agreement reached.

The Nuclear Test Ban Treaty of July 25, 1963, was the first treaty between the East and West on any major cold-war issue since the Austrian State Treaty of 1955. While to some observers the Test Ban Treaty was a "historical breakthrough," to President Kennedy it was merely a "first step toward reason, away from war." The treaty had been in the making for over five years. The main difficulty had been to find a generally acceptable system of inspection against underground testing. When that proved impossible, the final treaty limited the test ban to the atmosphere, outer space, and under water. This, of course, made it less effective. Another flaw was the fact that the treaty was not signed by all actual or potential members of the "nuclear club." The initial signatories—America, Britain, and Russia—were later joined by most other countries, with the notable exceptions of France and Communist China. Both of them were in the process of becoming nuclear powers in their own rights. The fact that two major powers, one each from the free and Communist worlds, had thus deserted their respective camps in order to go it alone, was significant. It showed that the ties that once united the members of the two power blocs had become loosened. This dissolution of the Eastern and Western alliance systems is often seen as one of the major contributing causes to the relaxation of East-West tensions in recent years.

THE DISSOLUTION OF THE SOVIET AND WESTERN BLOCS

We have already discussed the changed relationship between Russia and her eastern European satellites (see pp. 129–35) as well as her struggle with Red China for leadership in the Communist world (see p. 149). The rift between Moscow and Peking poses a major threat to Communist unity which thus far has been at least outwardly maintained. Until the Cuban crisis in 1962 the Russians and Chinese had been guarded and indirect in their attacks upon each other; since then they have become quite outspoken in their mutual denunciations. Both Khrushchev and Mao Tse-tung made no secret of the fact that each would like to see the other overthrown by Communist factions more to their liking. Russia still holds the upper hand within the Communist world, with most of eastern Europe (including Yugoslavia) and Outer Mongolia supporting Khrushchev's policy of competitive coexistence. Red China is supported firmly only by North Korea, North Vietnam, and Albania. But in recent years both Romania and Cuba, once loyal followers of Moscow, have established additional ties with Peking and can at best be called neutral. The division of the Communist world, finally, is not restricted to purely Communist countries, but runs through Communist parties everywhere. The picture of a monolithic Communist bloc, as it existed until the late 1950's, is definitely a thing of the past.

Disintegration within the Communist camp is matched by disintegration within the free, Western world. Here the situation is more complex. Some differences among its members, such as occasional disagreements between the United States and Great Britain (see p. 45), never seriously weakened the effectiveness of the Western alliance system. In other cases, such as the dispute between Greece and Turkey over Cyprus, or the rapprochement between Pakistan and Red China, the threat to Western unity has been more serious. The most disruptive influence within the Western camp has come from France. In an understandable effort to revive his nation's prestige and to reassert Europe's influence within the Western world, President de Gaulle has followed a course which, to all intents and purposes, has taken France out of such key Western defense organizations as NATO and SEATO and has seriously weakened the movement toward European unity (see p. 50). As in any alliance, the members of the Western bloc were ready to forget their differences as long as they were faced by a common threat, in this case communism. As this threat has seemed to decrease, disunity has once more come to the fore. Just as Russia's leadership today is being challenged by Red China, so is America's leadership being challenged by France.

The result of the, at least partial, dissolution of the Eastern and Western power blocs has been to introduce an element of mobility into international affairs that would have been unthinkable ten or even five years ago. The days when each crisis would find the world divided into two ideological camps are over. Mobility, in turn, has brought uncertainty. Neither the United States nor Russia can count any longer on the unquestioning allegiance of more than a handful of their staunchest allies. It is this uncertainty, together with the realization that a nuclear war knows no victors, which may be partly responsible for the recent moderation in Russian policy.

Such moderation, however, is not rooted in fear or a feeling of inferiority. On the contrary, the Soviet Union's spectacular triumphs in the race for outer space and its industrial achievements have confirmed the belief of most Russians in the superiority of the Communist system. The result of this confidence is a cocksureness in which the Russians see nothing incongruous about telling the West to change its ways or get "its knuckles rapped," while at the same time assuring the world that Russia is sincerely interested in peaceful coexistence. Time, the Russians have boasted repeatedly, is on the side of communism. A Communist victory over capitalism no longer depends solely on military superiority, it is certain to come as the result of peaceful economic competition between the East and West. One of the most important demonstrations of this competitive coexistence is in the struggle for the allegiance of the world's underdeveloped and uncommitted nations. The main weapon in this struggle is economic aid to these countries.

AID TO UNDERDEVELOPED LANDS

The term "underdeveloped" applies not merely to the colonial regions recently liberated from foreign control, but to any area suffering from a low standard of living, including most of Latin America. It does not, furthermore, denote inherent poverty. As we have seen, many of the economically backward nations are rich in resources that, if developed, could bring great profits. Even in their present state the backward nations play an important role in the world's economy by contributing vital raw materials and markets for industrial exports. To help these countries develop their economic potentialities, therefore, is not merely a dictate of political necessity to gain support in the conflict between the free and Communist worlds. It is also a matter of economic self-interest for the more highly industrialized nations of western Europe and America.

The need to aid underdeveloped countries has become the more urgent because of the unprecedented population growth since 1945. In 1962 the world's total population passed the 3 billion mark, and this number is growing at the rate of 48 million per year, or 85 people per minute. The reason for this "population explosion" is not so much an increase in the birth rate as a decline in infant mortality and the death rate. Official birth-control programs have not been very effective, except in Japan and more recently in South America. If present trends continue, the world's population at the end of this century will be twice what it is today. The bulk of this increase will take place in Asia, Africa, and Latin America, whose populations will make up five-sixths of the total. Unless drastic steps are taken to curb this growth and to satisfy the economic needs of these vast masses, the poor will inherit the earth.

The development of economically backward regions must be attacked from two directions—through self-help and through outside aid. Where the will for self-improvement is lacking, no amount of foreign assistance will do much good. The responsibility for giving aid has been borne by all the advanced nations, although the United States has contributed the major share. We have already discussed the initiation of the Point Four Program by President Truman in 1949 (see p. 75). Its basic idea was to give technical assistance supplemented by financial aid. Compared to the billions spent each year on military aid, the funds appropriated to the International Cooperation Administration (ICA) for Point Four have been small. Even so, the accomplishments of the Point Four Program in such areas as public health, agriculture, and education have been impressive. More recently the American Peace Corps has also become an effective agency for providing technical assistance. The United States also has been a major contributor to the UN Technical Assistance Program, as well as to such regional schemes as the Alliance for Progress in Latin America and the development programs of the Colombo Plan nations in South and Southeast Asia.

Aside from technical assistance the greatest need of underdeveloped countries has been for long-term investment in public works and basic industries. Here, too, the United States has taken the lead, in such joint undertakings as the International Bank for Reconstruction and Development (World Bank) and the International Finance Corporation, as well as in the purely American Export-Import Bank. But the economic aid given by these bodies, often in collaboration with private investors, tended to go to countries that already had some degree of industrialization, rather than to more backward regions. To help the latter, the United States government in 1957 established the Development Loan Fund. It was designed to make so-called soft loans on easier terms, including repayment in foreign currencies. A similar agency was the International Development Association (IDA), founded in 1960. Its members, besides the United States, were Canada, Japan, and the leading nations of western Europe. America had long been concerned over the failure of some of these countries—notably Japan and West Germany—to share their growing prosperity by shouldering some of the foreign-aid burden. Such a joint effort was needed especially in view of the economic offensive which the Communist bloc had begun to wage in the non-Communist world.

The beginnings of this Communist offensive go back to 1954, when the Soviet Union granted a first modest credit to Afghanistan. Next on the list of recipients were India, Egypt, Indonesia, Syria, and Iraq. The total aid, both economic and military, which the Communist bloc extended between 1954 and 1962 was estimated at 7 billion dollars. Compared to the more than 40 billion dollars which the United States alone spent over the same period for the underdeveloped countries, this Communist figure looked insignificant. But the effectiveness of the respective aid programs must not be measured simply by comparing the amounts spent by each side. Of equal, if not greater, importance was the way in which the money was spent.

While the Communists were careful to concentrate their aid on a few key countries, the free nations spread their funds thinly over a wide area. Communist aid, furthermore, was usually given in the form of long-term, low-interest loans rather than outright grants. This method seemed preferable to countries afraid of accepting handouts for fear of incurring political or military obligations. The Soviet Union claimed that its aid had "no strings attached." The fact that Communist strings were no less real for being less visible was usually overlooked. Finally, much of the economic assistance given by the Communist bloc was in the form of trade rather than aid. Through trade the poorer countries hoped to earn needed funds for economic development without becoming subject to "neo-colonialism," or "dollar diplomacy." Again this Communist emphasis on "trade, not aid" was deceptive, leading in many cases to the very dependence which the underdeveloped countries hoped to avoid.

Despite such hidden drawbacks the Communist aid program was able to score some notable successes. To meet this challenge, the United States in 1959 began revising its own foreign aid measures. From a past emphasis on military and bilateral aid, America now turned toward funneling more economic aid through international agencies like the Inter-American Development Bank, the International Development Authority, and the United Nations. In 1960 the UN Food and Agriculture Organization embarked on a five-year "Freedom from Hunger" campaign to raise the marginal living standards of more than half the human race. Such multilateral aid programs, since they are free from any political strings, are acceptable to all countries that refuse to join either side in the cold war but prefer to remain neutral.

In an effort to coordinate the various American aid programs, the Kennedy administration in 1961 established an Agency for International Development (AID) to take over the functions of the International Cooperation Administration and the Development Loan Fund. The tendency of AID in recent years has been to extend long-term loans rather than outright grants, and to concentrate American assistance in those underdeveloped countries, like Nigeria and India, that show the best returns from such aid. The cost of foreign aid runs high. For the decade of the sixties alone the total need of all the underdeveloped nations has been estimated at more than three hundred billion dollars. Most of this money could be provided through freer trade; but a substantial share will have to come from aid, grants, loans, and private investment. The world's underdeveloped countries present an immense reservoir of potential friends and economic partners. It is up to the West to recognize the value of trading with them and of investing in their future. If the West fails to do so, the East will.

COMPETITION FOR ARMS AND OUTER SPACE

Competitive coexistence between East and West was found in every sphere, from politics and economics to art and athletics. It was especially keen in the race for armaments and for control of outer space. When the Soviet Union first caught up with the United States by developing its own atomic and hydrogen weapons, it seemed as though a stage had been reached in which the threat of mutual annihilation would serve as an effective deterrent to war. But as each side began developing its defenses against nuclear attacks, and as military specialists began raising doubts about the annihilating effects of such attacks, the fear of nuclear war continued as great as ever. "Limited" wars along conventional lines, furthermore, were still possible. To be prepared for any kind of war, therefore, remained the overriding concern of East and West alike.

The comparative military strength of the Communist and free worlds has been the subject of much debate. It has varied, of course, at different times. As far as traditional forces are concerned, the picture has been fairly clear. The total armed forces of the Soviet Union, in excess of 3 million, have always outnumbered those of the United States which, in 1964, totaled 2.7 million. But while the bulk of Russia's military manpower is made up of ground forces, American manpower is more evenly divided among the three armed services. If we look at the total service manpower of the free and Communist worlds, moreover, the picture becomes more favorable. The total military forces of the Western alliance in 1964 were estimated at 7.9 million, as compared with 7.5 million for the Communist World. The latter figure includes the 2.5 million men of Communist China's armed forces whose collaboration with Russia appears dubious at best. On the sea and in the air the situation is equally reassuring. The Soviet Union has the second largest navy in the world, but except for submarines it is no match for the United States navy, let alone the combined navies of the Western alliance. America and Russia in 1964 each had about twenty nuclear-powered submarines. In the air the

United States likewise is considerably ahead of the Soviet Union in the total number of aircraft. America is especially strong in long-range bombers, while the Russians have more fighter and interceptor planes.

Taken as a whole, these are the forces that will play the major role in a limited, conventional war. During the 1950's American military planning had de-emphasized this type of warfare in favor of "massive retaliation," that is, full-scale nuclear war. Beginning in 1962, however, American strategic thinking changed. It now again envisages the possibility of "limited strategic war" against military and economic objectives rather than "massive retaliation" against enemy cities. The latter would merely bring retaliation in kind and thus lead to mutual annihilation. America's new strategy reintroduces an element of choice and flexibility that had been lacking in the "pushbutton" type of nuclear warfare. It also emphasizes the continued importance of conventional forces.

Still, the major concern of both sides in the cold war continues to be preparation for a possible nuclear showdown. Until the early 1960's it was feared that Russia was far ahead in the development of long-range missiles which may decide a nuclear war. Since then it has become clear that the "missile gap," if it ever existed, had been much exaggerated. In 1964 the Soviet Union had only a fraction of America's huge arsenal of over one thousand intercontinental ballistic missiles (ICBM's). Most of America's missiles are based on underground launching sites invulnerable to enemy attack. The Soviets still lead in intermediate- and medium-range ballistic missiles (MRBM's). These are a threat primarily to western Europe. But this threat is balanced by America's superiority in long-range delivery systems. Besides ICBM's these include missile-carrying long-range bombers and submarines. The Russians, too, have such submarines. But while the American Polaris is an intermediate missile that can be launched from under water, Russia's submarines carry only short-range missiles that must be launched from the surface.

With the perfection of long-range missiles carrying nuclear warheads, "pushbutton" warfare had arrived. Because of the element of surprise in such a war, air defense became a matter of foremost concern. The United States tackled this problem from two directions: by setting up early warning systems, such as the DEW line across Alaska and northern Canada, and by antiaircraft and antimissile defenses. By 1964 America had several surface-to-air missiles, like the Nike-Hercules and the Bomarc, for use against airplanes. The only weapon against ICBM's, however, the Nike-Zeus, was still under development. Little was known about Soviet air defenses other than fighter aircraft. Russia's cities, like those of the United States, are surrounded by antiaircraft installations. There have also been reports of two antimissile missile sites near Moscow and Leningrad.

The contest for military leadership between the United States and the Soviet Union was closely related to their competition for the conquest of outer space. The competition began when Russia put its first Sputnik into orbit on October 4, 1957. This feat was followed by America's launching of its first satellite on January 31, 1958. From there on the race continued, as the Russians put their first two cosmonauts into orbit in April and August, 1961, and the United States followed suit with its two manned orbital flights in 1962. Shortly thereafter the Soviets had two men orbiting the earth simultaneously; and in 1963 they repeated this simultaneous performance with a man and woman cosmonaut. In 1964, finally, the Soviet Union put a capsule containing three men into space. The Russians thus held the lead, with seven space flights and a total of 275 orbits as against America's four flights with a total of 34 orbits. America, however, had put a far greater number of objects into orbit and had gained more varied and valuable scientific information from such probes.

Russia's apparent leadership in the space race was of great propagandist value in the era of competitive coexistence. To catch up with and surpass the Russians, the Kennedy administration in 1961 launched an ambitious long-range program to land a man on the moon by 1970. This Apollo project will cost at least twenty billion dollars. Its proponents claim that its successful completion will not only enhance American prestige, but will also be of the greatest military value. Critics of the project, on the other hand, charge that its vast funds could be better employed in more urgent military and civilian programs. Such criticism gained momentum when Premier Khrushchev announced in 1963 that the Soviet Union was pulling out of the race to the moon. The Russians, it was feared, were concentrating on projects of more immediate military usefulness. In the wake of such criticism funds for the Apollo project have been reduced, and it has fallen behind schedule.

The American space and missile program has suffered from other handicaps, notably interservice rivalries. The army, navy, and air force each have their own missiles, while a separate civilian agency, the National Aeronautics and Space Administration (NASA) is in charge of developing high-thrust rockets for space flights. Soviet missile and rocket projects, in contrast, are reportedly concentrated under one authority, thus avoiding unnecessary duplication and expense. Because of the secrecy surrounding the interrelated competition for arms and outer space, it is impossible to reach any definite conclusion about the comparative strength of the two superpowers. This much is clear, however: Both sides have sufficient military power to strike a crippling or annihilating blow against the other; and each side is spending unprecedented sums on military and space programs to the detriment of more constructive peaceful purposes. The resulting "balance of terror" exposes mankind to a degree of tension unknown in any other age. The only possible relief from this tension is through disarmament.

ATOMS FOR WAR OR PEACE?

The question of disarmament, as we have seen, had come up at almost every East-West conference since 1945. The basic problem on each occasion turned out to be the control of nuclear weapons. The United States consistently proposed that disarmament proceed in stages, each stage accompanied by careful international inspection. The Soviet Union, with equal consistency, called for a complete ban on nuclear weapons, to be followed by some unspecified form of control. The need for disarmament, meanwhile, became more urgent as Great Britain, France, and finally Red China joined the ranks of the atomic powers. Britain exploded its first atomic bomb in 1952 and its first hydrogen bomb in 1957; France followed suit with its first atomic bomb in 1960; and China tested its first nuclear device in 1964. With technological development lowering the cost of nuclear weapons, the outlook was for other powers to join the "atomic club" at some future date.

There have been several agencies concerned with disarmament, from the UN Disarmament Commission that conducted negotiations through the 1950's, to the eighteen-nation Disarmament Conference that has been meeting in Geneva since 1962. These agencies have considered a wide range of proposals, from the American-sponsored Baruch Plan (see p. 28) to the Soviet Union's 1959 proposal for "general and complete disarmament." On none of these schemes has any agreement been reached. The basic issues throughout the negotiations have remained the same. The Soviet Union continues to demand the complete elimination of those military factors most dangerous to its security, including bombers, missiles, and overseas bases. Only after these forms of military power have been eliminated will the Russians consider some system of international inspection. The West, on the other hand, wants a carefully controlled, step-by-step arms reduction in which each side would reduce its strength proportionately, so that the balance of military power would always remain the same. While there has been no progress on these basic issues, some agreement has been reached on collateral issues. The "hot line" agreement and the Test Ban Treaty are examples. In the fall of 1963 the United States and the Soviet Union supported a UN resolution against placing nuclear weapons in orbit. In the spring of 1964 Russia, Great Britain, and America agreed to reduce the production of fissionable materials for nuclear weapons. These are small achievements, compared to the magnitude of the disarmament problem. But by helping to ease tension, they may contribute to a solution of the many political differences between the East and West that are the basic cause of the arms race.

Compared to the time and money spent in preparation for a nuclear war, the efforts to develop the peaceful uses of atomic energy have been meager. A first step in this direction was made with President Eisenhower's "atoms for peace" proposal in 1953. The United States subsequently offered to contribute fissionable materials to an international pool if other nations would follow suit. In addition America began making atomic fuels available to more than twenty-five countries. In 1956 both England and France started their first atomic power plants, and the six nations of the European Economic Community established the Euratom agency for the common development of atomic energy (see p. 62). In 1958 the United States entered upon a joint ten-year program of research and development with Euratom. The Soviet Union, meanwhile, began sharing its own atomic knowledge with its satellites and with Yugoslavia and Egypt.

In October, 1956, a UN Atoms for Peace Conference in New York established the International Atomic Energy Agency (IAEA) with headquarters in Vienna. Its purpose was to make available to less developed countries fissionable materials and nuclear equipment for peaceful projects. The fissionable materials were to be contributed by those countries that could spare them. To make sure that these materials were used for peaceful purposes only, a system of inspection was set up. The IAEA initiated programs of research and nuclear information and drafted health and safety rules for the use of nuclear fuels. The greatest progress in peaceful atomic development was in the field of electric power generation. Another promising area for research is the desalting of seawater. The United States has made increasing amounts of uranium 235 available for peaceful projects at home and abroad. In 1963 the United States and Russia initiated a cooperative program of nuclear research providing for a limited exchange of scientists and scientific information. In a message to the UN's third Atoms for Peace Conference in 1964 President Johnson hailed the atom as a "powerhouse for peace" and promised to share the fruits of American atomic research with the rest of the world. The infinite energy unlocked by such research promises to provide the means of ultimately insuring a decent living to all mankind.

THE FUTURE IN PERSPECTIVE

As the year 1964 neared its end, the outlook, as far as East-West relations were concerned, seemed more hopeful than at any time since 1945. At this point, while the world was awaiting the outcome of the national elections in Britain and the United States, events in Russia and Red China injected a new note of upheavel and uncertainty into international affairs. On October 15, 1964, Moscow curtly announced the dismissal of Khrushchev from his positions of leadership within the Soviet state and the Communist Party. The post of premier went to Alexei N. Kosygin, and the key post of party secretary went to Leonid I. Brezhnev. The following day, October 16, Peking announced the successful explosion of Red China's first atomic device.

Taken together, these two events may usher in a new phase in the cold war. Red China's entrance into the "nuclear club" had been foreseen for some time, and most observers agree that it will take many years before the Chinese will become serious contenders in the atomic race. The changes in Russia, on the other hand, appear more serious. The new leaders of the Soviet Union owed their earlier rise to the man they now replaced. The question is: Will they also continue the policies of their predecessor? Their initial policy statements have been to this effect. Yet judging from previous shake-ups in the Kremlin, especially after the death of Stalin, it is by no means certain that the new men are here to stay, and that "collective leadership" will last. Nor is there any assurance, considering developments in China, that the split between Moscow and Peking, which indirectly has helped to ease East-West tensions, will continue. It remains to be seen, therefore, how long the present stage of competitive coexistence in East-West relations will last, whether it will give way to new cold-war battles, or whether it will eventually ease into genuine cooperation. In the meantime continued armed watchfulness combined with readiness to negotiate on any issue that separates the free from the Communist worlds must remain the basis of Western policy.

The course of world history since 1945, which we have followed here in outline, has been unique in many ways. Never before have there been more startling discoveries and developments in science and technology; never before have so many people gained their freedom in so brief a span of time; never before has a generation been faced with the exciting and frightening alternatives which the atom has put before us: to live more comfortably, if not more happily, in an increasingly crowded world thanks to the peaceful use of atomic energy; or to use that same energy to blow to pieces the very planet on which we live.

We have lived so long with the fear of war that we have grown quite used to it. But should that fear be suddenly removed, people the world over would experience a wonderful feeling of relief. To ease the burden of preparedness would also release immense sources of energy that could be put to more peaceful and constructive uses. Somehow, it seems, ways and means must be found to break the vicious circle of large armaments leading to mutual suspicion, and mutual suspicion leading to still larger armaments.

It is often held that the best means of avoiding world destruction would be the creation of an effective world government. The beginnings of such an organization exist, of course, in the United Nations. That world organization, as we have seen, has rendered valuable services in settling some minor international crises and in making its moral weight felt in some major ones. But the United Nations is still far from being a true world government. As long as self-interest continues to be the guiding principle of nations, and as long as the stronger powers are unwilling to create a world organization commanding greater strength than they do, an effective supranational government remains a pious hope. Apart from this continued hold of nationalism, the ideological split between the East and West makes the formation of a world state still more difficult.

Some people feel that we tend to overemphasize the role of the two superpowers, Russia and the United States. After all, they include only about one-seventh of the world's population. Certainly the gradual emergence of the former colonial regions, whose peoples constitute a majority in the world, should profoundly alter the present picture. But it would be wishful thinking to expect the influence of this potential "third force" to be necessarily for the better. The position of neutralism taken by most of these new nations is often defended as impartial and benevolent. Yet such a position is more often dictated by weakness and by the needs of the moment. It is not suggested that the colored peoples of the world will some day stand against the white peoples. But the nationalism shown in recent years by Arabs and Africans, Asians and Latin Americans, does not hold much promise that the emancipation of the colonial peoples will bring us any closer to the ideal of an enlightened world government.

The inability of people, then, to solve their differences through some form of supranational government, and the possibility that these differences, if unresolved, may result in a major catastrophe are the main reasons why our present world is such a fearful place to live in. It would be false optimism to assume that this situation will improve within the near future. But such an environment does not mean that we cannot at least try to lessen the dread in which we are forced to live. Most people make the mistake of viewing the world's problems too narrowly and rigidly, ignoring or excluding alternatives and overlooking the possibility of a middle course. We live in an age in which the word "compromise" is under suspicion as being synonymous with "appeasement." But it is only through compromise, through a process of give and take, that misunderstandings can gradually be eliminated, differences ironed out, and fears made smaller. Such lessening of tensions will be slow work, requiring imagination, patience, good will, and continued watchfulness. Yet to ignore the possibility of thus slowly reducing the differences that today divide the world would be a fatalistic admission that man has lost control over his own fate.

Suggestions For
Further Reading

THE SUGGESTIONS GIVEN BELOW PRESENT ONLY
a small fraction of the many books available on recent world affairs.
Because of the rapidly moving course of events, the emphasis is on
the most recent works. All titles are available in paperback.

1. *The Cold War*

Bailey, S.D. *The United Nations—A Short Political Guide.* New
York: Praeger, 1963.
Gross, E.A. *The United Nations: Structure for Peace.* New York:
Harper, 1962.
Kennan, G.F. *American Diplomacy 1900–1950.* New York: Men-
tor, 1952.
Kennan, G.F. *Russia and the West under Lenin and Stalin.* New
York: Mentor, 1962.

Leckie, R. *Conflict: The History of the Korean War 1950–1953.* New York: Avon, 1962.
Lukacs, J. *A History of the Cold War.* Garden City, N. Y.: Doubleday, 1962.
Merkl, P.H. *The Origin of the West German Republic.* New York: Oxford, 1963.
Seton-Watson, H. *Neither War nor Peace: The Struggle for Power in the Postwar World.* New York: Praeger, 1961.
Snell, J.L. *Illusion and Necessity—The Diplomacy of Global War 1939–1945.* Boston: Houghton Mifflin, 1963.
Spanier, J. *American Foreign Policy since World War II.* New York: Praeger, 1962.

2. The Reassertion of Western Europe

Beloff, M. *The United States and the Unity of Europe.* New York: Random House, 1963.
Boyd, F. *British Politics in Transition 1945–63.* New York: Praeger, 1964.
Freymond, J. *Western Europe Since the War—A Short Political History.* New York: Praeger, 1964.
Furniss, E.S., Jr. *France, Troubled Ally—De Gaulle's Heritage and Prospects.* New York: Praeger, 1960.
Grosser, A. *The Federal Republic of Germany.* New York: Praeger, 1964.
Kitzinger, V.W. *The Politics and Economics of European Integration: Britain, Europe, and the United States.* New York: Praeger, 1963.
Krause, L.B., ed. *The Common Market—Progress and Controversy.* Englewood Cliffs, N.J.: Prentice-Hall, 1964.
Lichtheim, G. *The New Europe—Today and Tomorrow.* New York: Praeger, 1963.
Shanks, M., and Lambert, J. *The Common Market Today and Tomorrow.* New York: Praeger, 1962.
Spearman, D. *Democracy in England.* New York: Crowell-Collier, 1962.

3. The United States and Its Good Neighbors

Albertson, D. *Eisenhower as President.* New York: Hill & Wang, 1963.
Alexander, R.J. *Today's Latin America.* Garden City, N.Y.: Doubleday, 1962.

Berle, A.A. *Latin America—Diplomacy and Reality*. New York: Harper, 1962.
Dickey, J.S., ed. *The United States and Canada*. Englewood Cliffs, N.J.: Prentice-Hall, 1964.
Draper, T. *Castro's Revolution—Myths and Realities*. New York: Praeger, 1962.
Dreier, J.C. *The Organization of American States and the Hemisphere Crisis*. New York: Harper, 1962.
Goldman, E. *The Crucial Decade and After: America 1945–1960*. New York: Random House, 1960.
Matthews, H.L., ed. *The United States and Latin America*. Englewood Cliffs, N.J.: Prentice-Hall, 1963.
Nicolson, N.L. *Canada in the American Community*. Princeton, N.J.: Van Nostrand, 1963.
Rovere, R.H. *The American Establishment and Other Reports, Opinions and Speculations*. New York: Harcourt, Brace, 1962.
Szulc, T. *The Winds of Revolution—Latin America Today and Tomorrow*. New York: Praeger, 1963.

4. The Soviet Union and Its Satellites

Brumberg, A., ed. *Russia under Khrushchev*. New York: Praeger, 1962.
Brzezinski, Z.K. *The Soviet Bloc—Unity and Conflict*. New York: Praeger, 1963.
Crankshaw, E. *Khrushchev's Russia*. Baltimore: Penguin, 1962.
Crankshaw, E. *The New Cold War: Moscow v. Pekin*. Baltimore: Penguin, 1963.
Djilas, M. *Conversations with Stalin*. New York: Harcourt, Brace, 1962.
Fischer-Galati, S. *Eastern Europe in the Sixties*. New York: Praeger, 1963.
Floyd, D. *Mao against Khrushchev—A Short History of the Sino-Soviet Conflict*. New York: Praeger, 1963.
Kulski, W.W. *The Soviet Regime—Communism in Practice*. Syracuse, N.Y.: Syracuse University Press, 1963.
Leonhard, W. *The Kremlin since Stalin*. New York: Praeger, 1962.
Mehnert, K. *Soviet Man and his World*. New York: Praeger, 1962.

5. The End of Colonialism

Barnett, A.D. *Communist China in Perspective*. New York: Praeger, 1962.

Berger, M. The Arab World Today. Garden City, N.Y.: Doubleday, 1964.

Boyd, R.G. Communist China's Foreign Policy. New York: Praeger, 1962.

Burke, F.G. Africa's Quest for Order. Englewood Cliffs, N.J.: Prentice-Hall, 1964.

Butwell, R. Southeast Asia Today and Tomorrow. New York: Praeger, 1961.

Campbell, R.D. Pakistan: Emerging Democracy. Princeton, N.J.: Van Nostrand, 1963.

Cremeans, C.D. The Arabs and the World—Nasser's Arab Nationalist Policy. New York: Praeger, 1963.

Emerson, R. From Empire to Nation—The Rise to Self-Assertion of Asian and African Peoples. Boston: Beacon, 1962.

Fairbank, J.K. The United States and China. New York: Viking, 1963.

Higgins, B., and Higgins, J. Indonesia: The Crisis of the Millstones. Princeton, N.J.: Van Nostrand, 1963.

Jacobs, D.N., and Baerwald, H.H., eds. Chinese Communism—Selected Documents. New York: Harper, 1963.

Lamb, B.P. India: A World in Transition. New York: Praeger, 1963.

Lewis, J.P. Quiet Crisis in India—Economic Development and American Policy. Garden City, N.Y.: Doubleday, 1964.

London, K., ed. New Nations in a Divided World—The International Relations of the Afro-Asian States. New York: Praeger, 1963.

Maki, J.M. Government and Politics in Japan. New York: Praeger, 1962.

Moussa, P. The Underprivileged Nations. Boston: Beacon, 1963.

Ward, B. The Rich Nations and the Poor Nations. New York: Norton, 1962.

6. Competitive Coexistence

Birrenbach, K. The Future of the Atlantic Community—Toward European-American Partnership. New York: Praeger, 1963.

Black, E.R. The Diplomacy of Economic Development and Other Papers. New York: Atheneum, 1963.

Boyd, A. An Atlas of World Affairs, 5th ed. New York: Praeger, 1964.

Boyd, A. United Nations: Piety, Myth, and Truth. Baltimore: Penguin, 1962.

Buchan, A. *NATO in the 1960's—The Implications of Interdependence*. New York: Praeger, 1963.

Clubb, O.E., Jr. *The United States and the Sino-Soviet Bloc in Southeast Asia*. Washington, D.C.: Brookings, 1963.

Cottrell, A.J., and Dougherty, J.E. *The Politics of the Atlantic Alliance*. New York: Praeger, 1964.

Dallin, A. *The Soviet Union at the United Nations*. New York: Praeger, 1962.

Hauser, P.M., ed. *The Population Dilemma*. Englewood Cliffs, N.J.: Prentice-Hall, 1963.

Martin, L.W., ed. *Neutralism and Nonalignment—the New States in World Affairs*. New York: Praeger, 1963.

Mosely, P.E. *The Kremlin and World Politics*. New York: Random House, 1960.

Pentony, D.E. *China the Emerging Red Giant—Communist Foreign Policies*. San Francisco: Chandler, 1962.

INDEX

Acheson, Dean, 74, 77, 78
Adenauer, Konrad, 22, 52 ff., 183
Adoula, Cyrille, 170–71
Afghanistan, 197
Afro-Asian Economic Conferences, 172
Afro-Asian People's Solidarity Conferences, 172
Agency for International Development (AID), 198
Albania, 22, 26, 112, 126, 130, 133, 135, 149, 194
Algeria, 47, 48–50, 165, 173
All-African People's Conferences, 173
Alliance for Progress, 99, 197
Allied Control Council, 5, 12, 19
Angola, 59, 167
Ankara Treaty, 116, 134
ANZUS Treaty, 31, 34, 35
Arab League, 163, 165
Argentina, 35, 92, 93

Asian-African conferences, 172 ff.
Assembly of Captive European Nations (ACEN), 113
Association of Southeast Asia (ASA), 157
Ataturk, Mustafa Kemal, 161
Atlantic Charter, 4, 17
Atomic bomb, 11, 12, 28, 36, 45, 149, 191, 193, 202, 204
Atomic disarmament, 28, 193, 202 ff. See also Disarmament
Atomic Energy Commission (UN), 28
"Atoms for Peace," 181, 203 ff.
Attlee, Clement, 11 ff., 41
Australia, 31, 35, 44, 138, 157
Austria, 60, 63, 64: peace treaty with, 60, 118, 182

Baghdad Pact, 166
Balewa, Sir Abubakar T., 138

213